The Freelance Writer's Handbook

PAUL KERTON

WITH

Colin Greenland

EBURY PRESS
LONDON

To Dawn. Despite whom this book was written.

Special thanks to Deirdre McSharry for getting me started. And to Linda Kelsey, for fine tuning.

Published by Ebury Press
Division of The National Magazine Company Ltd
Colquhoun House
27–37 Broadwick Street
London W1V 1FR

First impression 1986

ISBN 0 85223 555 0 (hardback)
0 85223 594 1 (paperback)

Designed by Ted McCausland
Cover design by Peter Bridgewater

Phototypeset by MS Filmsetting Ltd,
Frome, Somerset

Printed in Great Britain at The Bath Press, Bath, Avon

CONTENTS

THE PROFESSIONAL WRITER

Why Write?

> 'I've no desire to be Tolstoy. I simply want to earn a living.'
>
> *Incipient freelance writer*

> 'I got into writing because I had nothing else to do. It ain't something you talk about—it's something you do. One thing I do know: the more you learn about writing, the tougher it gets.'
>
> SAM SHEPARD

> 'I'm a born writer. I just wrote. I used to compose poems inside my head even before I could read or write. When I read my first book, I was hooked. I became a writer because I wanted to recreate this magical thing called a book.'
>
> COLLEEN MCCULLOUGH

There's far more glamour and mystique surrounding the business of writing than it deserves. After all, everyone who's not actually illiterate can and does write—a diary, a postcard home, a note for the milkman—yet there are some of us who take this basic skill and turn it into a livelihood.

Most of us are anonymous, or might as well be as far as the people who read us are concerned. Journalists have their words attributed to the publication they work for ('The *Express* reckons Russia's behind it'), while even novelists are less important to many readers than the category of books they write: romances, war stories, spy novels. That is, until they begin to emerge from the herd and nose into the bestseller lists. Then the machinery of fame takes over, and writers become their own categories ('Have you got any more Catherine Cookson?'). Their names are printed in larger letters *above* the titles of their books. The sums they earn are mentioned in colour supplement profiles and gossip columns. They appear on TV chat shows. They become media personalities. The only act of theirs that isn't public property, ironically enough, is the physical act of setting words on paper—or, increasingly, on floppy disc. So the mystique is deepened, the glamour enhanced.

This book will not necessarily make you into Leo Tolstoy, or Catherine Cookson. But if you're already writing, and the idea of selling what you write as a freelance appeals to you, the interviews, insights and advice here will show you how it's done.

If you have something to say and can transfer those thoughts from brain to paper, then you're in business. That is, if you can present the result well enough and are not afraid to put yourself forward. Writing is between you and your sheet of paper; but selling what you write requires you to interact with a system which exists outside you. Sometimes its indifference will seem almost personal, like a conspiracy preventing you from getting into print. You will need great persistence, and the ability to cope with frustration and doubt. But after reading this book, you will be better prepared for the realities of the task; and, with a bit of luck, you might even find yourself writing for a living.

What to Write

What do you write? What *can* you write? The old adage 'write what you know' is all very well, but if you don't know very much then you're stuck. Why confine yourself to what you know already when part of the professional writer's job is to go and find out what things are like, often at someone else's expense? Obviously this is most true of the news reporter sent out at five minutes' notice to cover a story—but it's equally true of a journalist who's convinced an editor they simply must run a piece on potholing; or of an interviewer setting out to meet Tina Turner; or, by extension, of a reviewer sitting down with a first novel by a complete unknown. The popular press gives everyone such an appetite for novelty that, if you're going to develop and broaden as a writer, you will need to acquire new experiences and new techniques as you go.

The old-fashioned image of the writer as recluse, locked in some shabby garret, communing only with the muse, will be of little use to you. Certainly you'll need solitude and privacy when it comes to thinking up words and setting them down, especially if you're writing fiction; but succeeding commercially isn't something you can do alone. Much depends on perfecting the social skills to deal with editors, other writers and people in the business; on developing the confidence to go where you need to pick up the material you want; on building and sustaining a reputation. Nevertheless, none of this will work if you're not writing what you're good at.

The other adage is 'Everybody has a book in them'. Your professional career will depend on the fact that not everybody can bring that book out. You may think your idea or even your own life would make a wonderful novel; but do you have the necessary skills and faculties to get it down in a form that publishers will recognize and people will want to read? Would you be better off working your way up to the full-length work of fiction by concentrating on short stories first? How will you cope with the dearth of outlets for short stories in Britain? Can you do useful work, work that interests you and teaches you something, within the confines of the romantic form published by women's magazines in large quantities every week?

Are you more interested in facts? Can you spot a good story, an intriguing character or fascinating subject, research it thoroughly and write it up accurately and attractively? Or do you already have a speciality which you feel you could readily turn into a strong and reliable source of copy?

Editors have to have contacts with large numbers of writers and know what each one is useful for. Consequently, they like to pigeonhole people. If, after a few years, you can get yourself into the position where your name is inextricably connected with your favourite subject in your publisher's mind, then you're assured of work, even of some measure of renown. But do beware—the reason I never specialized was that I couldn't think of anything more boring than writing about one subject day in, day out. I know quite a few beauty editors who say ominous things like 'God, it's soul-destroying just writing about beauty.'

Personally, I think versatility is the key to (a) making a decent living from writing, and (b) enjoying doing it. It is possible to change your style to suit different publications without losing your personal voice. Having the freedom to be clever, funny, sympathetic, critical, wicked, sarcastic and vulnerable by turns is vital if you're not to grow stale. Beware, though, of spreading yourself too thin. One month in 1984 I had nine articles in nine different magazines on the news-stands, ranging from *Penthouse* to *Cosmopolitan*. That was a great feeling, but the effort involved in dealing with nine different editors, providing them with nine different ideas written in nine different styles, was exhausting. In the end, the thinner you spread yourself, the more your work suffers as you fail to attend to any one area properly.

It's much better, especially if you are going to specialize on one topic, to cultivate three good publications. Three will keep you flexible without the risk of falling over trying to keep too many in the air at once. And remember: you always need somewhere else to go. No matter how good and stable your relationship with an editor, there will come a time when (a) you will fall out; (b) your usefulness to that magazine will come to an end; or (c) that editor gets fired or moves on.

Specialists Talking

When the home computer boom happened in the early 1980s, magazines for the consumer sprang up all over the place. People like Keith Bowden, a polytechnic lecturer, and Valerie Buckle, a full-time university student, were well placed to take advantage of a brand new market.

Valerie Buckle
At the beginning, the way we saw it, what people were doing was rushing to publish a computer magazine and make a lot of money. They'd get the first two issues out, then think: 'Help! Who's going to write the magazine? We don't know anything about the market, or about the computers themselves.' You didn't have to be a good journalist, or know about a whole wide range of aspects of computers. They just wanted somebody who had access to

their particular model to write copy for them. The magazines at that time were geared to people who didn't know very much about computers anyway.

Keith Bowden _____

I started pretty well at the beginning of the boom, about 1982, with no particular background as a writer. I was very enthusiastic about the Commodore 64, and wrote to *Personal Computer News* enthusing. I got a reply from a publisher who was looking for people to write books on various kinds of computer. From my response to this machine, he thought I was suitable. He didn't want to see anything I'd written. He just grabbed me, contracted me, and gave me three months to do it in, because he wanted to get the book out as soon as possible.

Freelance journalist Peter Knight is someone who decided to specialize 'out of necessity'.

66 I wasn't making enough money writing mainstream, general-purpose articles, and there seemed to be a growing demand for writers who could interpret technology for anyone to understand. It was a subject I was already interested in. What happened was the *Financial Times* was looking for someone to write their tech stuff for a new project; and I was in a position to say, Yes, I can do it. I took a month off and studied everything I could on the new technology – and I think this is important. Many freelancers don't look farther ahead than their next cheque. For them, taking a month off would be sacrilege, but for me it bore fruit. Once you know the subject you can churn the stuff out an awful lot quicker, and even regurgitate the same thing for different markets. My money has increased threefold. It's such a relief to be earning decent money. 99

Lorna Bourke writes for *The Times* business pages and *Money* magazine. It's not an area she had expected to specialize in when she started out as a journalist.

66 I originally wanted to write about the theatre, films and the ballet: things I was interested in. But there were too many people wanting to do that. I knew nothing then about money, but it became obvious that there was a huge demand for personal finance articles. Money is quite a technical subject, but it wasn't too difficult to learn. It was purely a journalistic skill: knowing where to get your information, and who to talk to. If someone offered me a gardening column at a greatly inflated salary, I would be a gardening expert tomorrow. 99

branching out

'The only way to learn is to write, to write for years and years and years, from childhood. What you can't do is come out of school at age 16 and think, I'd quite like to be a writer. You can't. You are a writer already. George Bernard Shaw said: "When I was a child, I always wanted to be a pirate captain. I never wanted to be a writer, because I always was. It was like the taste of water in my mouth." And that's true. If you *aren't* a writer, you never will be.'

KIM NEWMAN, *freelance writer and critic*

Beyond journalism, if you have the contacts, you can find yourself lucrative work in advertising and public relations, like Paul Kincaid.

❝I used to be a copywriter for a·holiday firm. I wanted another job, so I wrote around the business, until another firm said, 'We don't have a job for you, but if you're interested in freelance work, we have plenty of that.' Now I write holiday brochures, direct mail letters, advertising copy, audio-visual scripts. There's a lot of freelance work in advertising copywriting, as in design, and the rates are really pretty good. I'll estimate a job will take me, say, four days, and quote them £100 a day. If I do it in three, I don't tell them it took me a day less! But if it takes me five, I forfeit that extra £100.

'I don't think anybody could go into freelance advertisement writing without having had some experience in the industry. But if you're already working as a freelance writer, advertising might be a place to try for extra income.

You have to be very flexible, and you can't have *a* style. Your name doesn't appear! Writing to length is also vital—and it's not "500 words", it's "50 lines, 36 characters per line".❞

How To Write

No one can tell you how to write. There are no principles guaranteed to make words appear on the paper, and no foolproof methods of ensuring that once they do appear, they will continue to do so.

That's not to say it's all magic. Writing, and particularly commercial writing, doesn't necessarily require inspiration. What it does require, whether it's the directions on an aerosol or *War and Peace*, is a modicum of talent, and some sort of discipline.

finding a discipline

Disciplines vary. Some writers require the stability of an artificial routine, and sit at their desks from nine to five like everybody else. Others work at night, when the phone won't ring and no one will be around to disturb them. The science fiction writer Frederik Pohl has a 'self-imposed regime of defacing four pages of clean paper with writing every day of my life'.

You may find it useful to set yourself a target of so many words, or so many hours a day. Another SF writer, John Stith, has a full-time job teaching maths. He began with a target of an hour a day spent writing fiction. Finding that difficult to manage, he cut it down, to half an hour, and finally to twenty minutes. That, he discovered, was practicable. It was just enough time to get interested, but too short to achieve much. So the twenty minutes started to expand. John began to put other things off, or get them out of the way beforehand. Eventually he was writing for two hours a day. He kept that up, and now has two novels in paperback.

Disciplines need not be regular. Some writers potter around for weeks and months producing nothing very visible, then disappear for a couple of months, type frenziedly day and night, and return at the end of it exhausted, but clutching a completed manuscript.

Choose a discipline that's right for you, and right for the work you're doing. Resign yourself to the fact that only *you* can do it, and that your best friends are a typewriter, a good chair and a blank sheet of paper.

putting it down on paper

Many writers admit to a pathological fear of that blank piece of paper. Most agree that having a deadline helps wonderfully. If someone else is expecting you to come up with something, and especially if they're relying on you to do it and you know there's a cheque at the end, you tend to produce results. But until then, writing without a commission, you really are on your own.

A common agony for the amateur is: 'If I can't get the first sentence, I can't get going'; or, conversely: 'I've got my first sentence, but I can't get any further.' The best advice you can have is to write down everything – *everything* – words, thoughts, half-thoughts, half-sentences, clever phrases, notes and queries, in any form and any order. Unload your brain. At least now you're writing *something*. What's more, you're thinking rapidly and fluently. Three-quarters of what you've got down on paper may eventually be scrapped, but at least it's all there *on* the paper for you to go over, not just in your head, or just out of your head because you thought of it a moment ago but didn't *write it down*.

Out of the jumble will come the logical order of what you want to say—including a title and that precious first sentence.

For example, you may be struck with the idea for an article on sex in society—something everyone knows a bit about. Divorce statistics are soaring. People you know seem to be sabotaging their relationships. There are more *kinds* of sex these days. From some viewpoints, it looks like a disaster. Disaster, that may be a useful word.

By now you should be writing.

```
Divorce on the increase.  Disaster?

Pat & Jo    }
Mike & Mandy   }  seem to be sabotaging their relationships.
* More kinds of sex: a) living w. someone
                     b) marriage
                     c) sleep around
                     d) single (respectable) - celibacy
                     e) straight or gay?
WHATEVER HAPPENED TO MATING???

Sexual confusion or is it social confusion.  Sex has
never been more sophisticated than it is today.

Reasons?  1 - contraception
          2 - easy divorce
          3 - busier social lives - even the unemployed:
                                        more leisure!
          4 - old moral standards dropped
          5 - male/female roles not so frozen
* it's all more like a board game or something.  bed & board
                                                    game?
```

```
all the singles I know seem to be
waiting for somebody to come along
and fulfil their lives.  Are there
any happy singles?
```

Go on until you know what you want to say, and where to
start. Then write a rough draft of it. Don't worry about
polish: that comes later.

Now you should have something that looks like this:

```
      THE MODERN MATING DISASTER

The mating game has never been more sophisticated than
it is today.  Safer contraception, busier social lives,
plummeting morals and a thawing of male/female relations
have all made the Mating Game more sophisticated and
much easier to play than ever before.  The very fact
that there are now so many choices available - to be
respectably single, to live with someone, to marry, to
be gay - have made playing the game that much more
difficult.  Confused - don't worry, so is everybody
else.  The Mating Game holds more contradictions than
a political manifesto.
```

Now you can get to work boiling it down. Remember it's going to have to persuade people to read it in the first place, regardless of whether they end up agreeing with you or not. So, cut out the repetitions and redundancies, and anything that sounds at all weak or irrelevant. Make sure your points and examples are in the best order. You should find yourself thinking along these lines:

THE MODERN MATING DISASTER

The mating game has never been more sophisticated than ① it is today. *Safer* contraception, busier social lives, ② ③ plummeting morals and a thawing of male/female relations

the majority of singles remain desperately ④ unhappy, fed-up and unfulfilled. have all made the Mating Game more sophisticated and much easier to play than ever before. The very fact ④ that there are *now* so many choices *available* - to be ⑤ respectably single, to live with someone, to marry, to ⑥ be (gay) - *have* made *playing the game* that much more *choosing an option* difficult. Confused don't worry, so is everybody /? ⑧ else. The Mating Game holds more contradictions than a political manifesto. ⑨

① So what? This is too pompous a statement and says nothing.
② 'Even with' sounds better.
③ 'Plummeting morals' is more important than 'busier social lives'.
④ This part of the sentence is total rubbish. Replace with ④
⑤ 'Now' and 'available' are redundant. If we have a choice, then we know choices are available.
⑥ Note the logical order of single; live with someone; marry. If I'd have put 'gay' first this would seem odd in a largely hetero mag.
⑦ 'Playing the game' says nothing. ⑧ Question mark since we're ending a question
⑨ I like the ending.

Now do it again. Check each word for important nuances; tinker with the fine detail.

more reliable ①
Even with *safer* contraception, plummeting morals, busier social lives and a thawing of male/female *hostilities* ①
relations, the majority of singles *men and women* ② remain desperately *or* ③ 'unhappy,' 'fed up *and* unfulfilled. The very fact that there are so many choices - to be respectably single, to live with someone, to marry, to be gay - has made *opting for one particular sexual lifestyle* choosing an option that much more difficult. ④ Confused? Don't worry, so is everybody else. The Mating Game holds more contradictions than a political manifesto.

① 'Safer' and 'relations' aren't the right words.
② Just being specific we are not talking about single giraffes.
③ Quotation marks add emphasis. 'Or' works better than 'and'.
④ It still didn't really say anything.

When time permits, leave a piece overnight or longer before the final revision. Delay adds clarity, and permits afterthoughts to surface.

This is how it appeared in print:

> *The Modern Mating Disaster*
>
> Even with more reliable contraception, plummeting morals, busier social lives and a thawing of male/female hostilities, the majority of single men and women remain desperately 'unhappy', 'fed up' or 'unfulfilled'. The fact that there are so many choices - to be respectably single, to live with someone, to marry, to be gay - has made opting for one particular sexual lifestyle that much more difficult. Confused? Don't worry, so is everybody else. The Mating Game holds more contradictions than a political manifesto.

If you're to work as a professional writer, this process of paring down and shaping up is what editors will do to your prose. It's vital that you learn to do it for yourself first.

● It helps you say exactly what you mean.

● It helps you fill your allotted word-length most effectively and economically.

● It gives your editor less work. Editors will always prefer the writer whose copy needs least attention.

Choosing the Tone

To be a star in freelance writing, you need a distinctive voice of your own, whether you're Sue Arnold or Bernard Levin. But that comes later. First you have to earn your place in the chorus line, by showing you know the basic routines and can handle all the necessary variations. We'll presume you wouldn't be contemplating a career as a writer if you didn't have a firm grasp of the English language—though you'd be surprised how many highly-paid freelance and staff journalists there are whose raw copy shows a blithe ignorance of the fundamentals of grammar and syntax, let alone spelling and punctuation. They get where they are by having a nose for news, an ear to the ground, an eye for style and (not to strain their anatomy further) the capacity to think fast and then work like demons. Only a comparison of what comes out of their typewriters with how it ends up in print shows that they're also dependent on battalions of dedicated and accurate sub-editors.

The moral is, it can be done. But you'll be much better advised to be reliable. And even if you're going to specialize, if you're not going to write yourself into a corner, you'll need to cultivate a versatility of tone. This you can do by listening, to the way people use words amongst themselves, and the way they're used on TV and radio; and by reading.

Don't go to the library shelf where books with titles like *The Use of English* and *Correct English* cluster. Whatever the academic qualifications of their authors, self-appointed custodians of the written word, they'll only lead you astray. What you must develop a sensitivity for is *living* language, complete with all its shifts and shuffles and short-cuts. Effective communication is primary. The rules must serve you, not the other way round. Remember being told in junior school English lessons never to begin a sentence with *and* or *but*? Now re-read the last paragraph.

'The question is,' said Humpty Dumpty, 'which is to be master—that's all.'

'New Journalism' of the 60s and 70s produced a style of highly contrived informality and spontaneity whose effects, at best, can be startlingly vivid. Here's the hyphen king, Tom Wolfe, starting a sentence with *And*:

❝And here they are, hyped up, turning bilious, nephritic, queer, autistic, sadistic, barren, batty, sloppy, hot-in-the-pants, chancred-on-the-flankers, leering, puling, numb—the usual in New York, in other words, and God know what else. ❞

(TOM WOLFE, *The Pump House Gang*)

There's a limit to the usefulness of this, especially now in the cooler, more cautious 80s. You can't even use it in the rock music press without a saving touch of irony:

❝REVELATION! REVELATION! ... James Dean Lives! Eddie Cochran's undead'n'kicking!!! SURF'S UP!! The Beach Bums have arisen—'*Out of the black/and into the blue/ROCK'N'ROLL will never die*' etc, etc, etc.
   SHIT! ... SHEEEYIT!!! ... Man, them Butthole Surfers are BAAAAAAAAAAAAAAAAAAAD (you're still only being paid for one word—Ed.). ❞

(*Review of the Butthole Surfers by 'New Delhi', NME,* 26 October 1985)

Be careful—a point is reached where loss of structure causes loss of meaning and when the reader becomes confused, he stops reading. Rock star Patti Smith ignored just about every rule of grammar in her book *Babel*. She doesn't even believe in starting a sentence with a capital letter. She signed my copy 'Total Abandon' which pretty much sums up the style and content of her book.

&& the distress of molten cadavers. the winds shift and my nostrils split. the rigid triangle the bolt of the hare. now racing now clinging to the giant wave. a bright green feel. molecules drop and accumulate in the shifting treasure box. **,,**

(PATTI SMITH, *Babel*)

No doubt some hallowed intellectual could provide a logical explanation of what Patti is trying to say, but most readers—if they were honest—would agree that it is abysmal stuff. She carried it *too* far. You have to be aware of a modicum of sentence structure in order for it to make enough sense for the reader to follow it.

The editor's decision *is* final, though a sub-editor may well make it first. When writing for any publication, you should have a clear idea of what its editor will accept, and of what's appropriate. The higher the brow of the journal, the greater the need for formal dignity, and for a prose style that requires immense and sober concentration from its reader:

&& This return to antiquity was not content merely to reproduce ancient models with archaeological authenticity (which was largely the extent of the second phase of classicism at the beginning of the nineteenth century), but it attempted to gain fundamental insights into the universal essence of architecture. **,,**

(KLAUS BUSMANN, *The Webb & Bower DuMont Guide to Paris*)

Considered and complexly-subordinated sentences like that will not cut much ice with browsers at the racks in airports, supermarkets and railway stations. Here, immediacy is everything:

&& When your young girl first discovers that boys are good for something besides writing in the snow and fixing her clock radio, she is at first surprised, then nervous, then pleased as punch. Short boys, tall boys, hairy boys, pimply boys, wimpy boys—she loves them all. **,,**

(CYNTHIA HEIMEL, *Sex Tips for Girls*)

The key to this is rhythm. The writing bounces along. Notice how she seduces you with a long introductory clause, then delivers three short, succinct phrases: pop, pop, pop. Unlike Busmann's, this is prose whose entire effect relies on its ability to reproduce in the mind's ear the linear flow of a speaking voice. No need for sustained concentration (the cliché term 'long-winded' means exactly that, speaking at length without pausing for breath); no need to re-read, no need to think.

This is not to say that all intellectual writing must be lifeless:

> 66 One of scholarship's more obvious last frontiers, a stretch of terrain that remains substantially uncolonised, is the borderland between those two uncomfortable neighbours, the history of art and the history of science. The reason for this neglect, of course, is that there are next to no scholars around who can penetrate the area with any confidence. The languages spoken in the territories that abut on it are so sharply different that little traffic has been able to develop. It has therefore been left a largely trackless wilderness, a wilderness in which the timid all too easily image a savage specialist lying in wait behind every boulder or bush. 99

> (DAVID ALLEN, 'Minute Particulars', *London Review of Books,* 6 February 1986)

Perhaps more importantly, lively journalism doesn't have to be (or pretended to be) brainless.

The Use of Pronouns

'Unless you have one great story to tell out of your own life, something like *Papillon,* then you are like an actor who does a series of different roles. You draw on what you know, but you conceal yourself. The more disguise the better!'

RACHEL INGALLS, *author of* Mrs Caliban

Unless *you* are the subject of the piece ('How I Sold My Own House'; 'A Grampian Childhood') beware of *I/me/mine.* Writing is a solitary business, and egocentricity is an occupational hazard. It's easy to lose sight of all those unknown people who are reading you and start filling the pages with 'I did this . . ., I did that . . ., in my opinion . . .'. The worst case of this is the interview feature which is crammed with the journalist's own musings, while the interviewee scarcely gets a word in edgeways! It's much better to attract readers to you by displaying your wit/insight/knowledge/creativity/ whatever to best advantage, rather than talking about yourself all the time. Don't forget some of those unknown readers will be editors on the lookout for new contributors.

However, it's not a good idea to try to hide yourself behind the bogus objectivity of *one.* 'One finds it hard to be complimentary about the French' does *not* disguise the fact that the difficulty is all your own, and you're not endearing yourself to anyone by offering to share it with the rest of us. *One* is tricky. It claims the authority of consensus, and if the reader doesn't grant it, merely sounds pompous. Why risk embarrassing yourself in print? If you can't turn the subject another way, be candid about your claims and admissions. It will certainly gain you more respect.

I'm writing this book in the present tense, and making free use of the word *you*. *You* makes assumptions about your reader—in this case, that we have a common interest, in writing for a living. Beware making assumptions that are unwarranted. I'm trying to avoid making assumptions about your sex, or your age, or your social background, because all kinds of people want to be writers. If this were an article for *Penthouse* or *My Weekly*, some of those assumptions could be made more readily. That aside, *you* has the advantage of being direct, establishing common ground, even a working relationship.

Adjectives and Adverbs

The brain easily gets over-sensitized to adjectives. Use too many and you end up conveying nothing.

> 66 *The long, winding road meandered through the heather-clad glacial valley. A disturbed moorhen gobbled loudly and then majestically spread its tawny wings before gracefully taking flight. The bracing rural air quickly filled my city-born lungs and it was enormously refreshing to be back in the tranquil countryside once more.* 99

English is a language with an enormous number of nouns but very few exact synonyms. Historically, we plundered most of them from other people's languages for specific purposes. Buy yourself the latest edition of *Roget's Thesaurus*—the one published by Longman, not anybody else's cheaper abridged edition—and learn to use it. Look for ways to telescope a string of adjectives into a more specific, or more suggestive, noun.

> 66 *The movie* The Neverending Story *features a dragon that looks more like a cross between a giant newt and a lovable, long-haired, soppy-eyed dog.* 99

There's no way of getting round *giant newt* because no such thing exists, but wouldn't *spaniel* do for the dog? This has the advantage of allowing your readers to attach their own associations to your description, which is always more convincing than telling somebody exactly what to think. More practically, it replaces six words with one: that's five more words you've just gained to say something else with, and still stay within your allotted word-limit.

One place where you will find adjectives piled up is in short, so-called 'capsule' reviews, such as this one of the film *Defence of the Realm* in the *New Statesman*.

> **❝** *Fumes of menace rise from David Drury's corrosive if erratic political chiller, written by Martin Stellman, reflecting current home-based concerns. Hoodwinked into disgracing awkward MP, tabloid reporter redemptively opens can of worms as Special Branch hovers.* **❞**

This is 'telegram' writing, packing maximum information and description into the smallest possible space. All the definite and indefinite articles have been left out, and nearly every word is forceful and evocative. It's a style which would become unreadable at greater length.

Clichés

Clichés are phrases that have become overused because they are extremely convenient, exact or just. An old fisherman's face *is* 'weather-beaten'. Extortionate price rises *are* 'daylight robbery'. Using a cliché is repeating what everyone has always said, and everyone is likely to agree with. But you're supposed to be a writer—somebody who's paid money to say new things, or old things in new ways.

Replace clichés with more original and vivid ways of saying things, unless there is something to be gained from their familiarity. On p. 14 wrote:

> **❝** *Considered and complexly-subordinated sentences like that will not cut much ice with browsers at the racks.* **❞**

Will not cut much ice with is definitely a cliché. But in that sentence it stands in contrast to *considered and complexly-subordinated sentences*—which is itself quite complex. *Always* avoid trite figures of speech such as:

She *rejoices in the name of* Lavinia.

Desmond Wilcox's *better half* is TV celebrity Esther Rantzen.

The football crowds *went their way homewards*.

These quaint expressions don't dress up your prose. They make it look naked and uncared-for.

'If you find yourself writing tired clichés like "as warm as toast", "as fresh as a daisy", or "cool as a cucumber" then you shouldn't be writing.'

MARCELLE D'ARGY SMITH
Features Editor,
Cosmopolitan

Punctuation

If you haven't already, you must stop thinking of punctuation marks as an arcane code enforced by unfriendly jurisdiction, like double yellow lines. Think of them as a battery of special effects at your command—cunning, convincing, and quite unobtrusive. Here are the top ten.

comma (,)

The comma is the most common way of breaking up a long sentence. It's a momentary pause and as a rough guide, put it where you would pause in spoken English.

> 66 *Stag nighters end up at least embarrassed, often diseased, arrested or, in some cases, stone cold dead.* 99

It can be used for a variety of purposes.

● Use a comma after a long introductory phrase:
But one notable aspect of the Heysel incident that few people commented on at the time was the absence of the famous hooligan stereotype, the skinhead.

● Use a comma if a sentence would be confusing without it:
The day before, I'd robbed the Bank of England

● Much argument is prompted as to whether or not to put a comma before an 'and', as in:
There were red ones, blue ones, and green ones.
or leave the comma out:
There were red ones, blue ones and green ones.

● Comma or no comma? I'd use one if the 'and' doesn't continue the series:
There were red ones, blue ones, and a bird ate the green ones.

● Use a comma to clarify a convoluted sentence:

> 66 *Chandris analyses, as far as possible, why we deposit fat, but has to admit, with the scientists, that there is as yet no full explanation for the fact that women tend to accumulate it on their rumps and legs; men on their torsos.* 99

Better still—don't write convoluted sentences!

semi-colon (;)

The semi-colon is a long pause, separating two main clauses, but keeping the elements more tightly linked than a full stop.

> 66 *She played the radio for him, but some of the programmes upset Garp; no one knew why.* 99

Notice how it makes that last clause sound more poignant.

full stop (.)

An end to the sentence. Period. A solid point which brings

the sentence to a close. It's also a good device to throw in at the beginning of a piece, after a single word, to let the reader savour the word, or concept, and drink in the impact:

> 66 *Impotence. The mere sound of the word is enough to make you go limp.* 99

dash (—)

The dash creates a dramatic pause to prepare for an expression needing strong emphasis:

> 66 *I styled Tina into a sex symbol—I made it happen. She'd stroke that mike—I told her to do that.* 99

Here used to back up the initial statement:

> 66 *The family's got it all—heroin addiction, alcoholism, a terrifyingly unpredictable atmosphere of punch-bag violence.* 99

It's also used in the middle of a sentence to slot in some clarifying or extra piece of information:

> 66 *Then I contacted his old record companies—labels like Kent, United Artists, and EMI (formerly Liberty)—to see if Ike was still collecting royalties.* 99

parentheses ( )

Brackets are used to pause quietly and drop in a few chatty asides not essential to your story:

> 66 *There were about six people crawling over and under my 1958 Wolseley (she hates Porsches).* 99

Or as a quick explanation:

> 66 *Cooper regarded the policeman with contempt (having already spent 15 years of his life behind bars), and then surrendered his weapon.* 99

Or as a vehicle for emphasizing absurdity:

> 66 *Vicars have had affairs with their congregation (Heavens!), they've stood in line at Cynthia Payne's brothel handing over Luncheon Vouchers for sex (Christ!), they've contracted AIDS (Lummy!) and one of them has has even been caught castrating dead bodies (Oh My God!).* 99

Use a dash and brackets sparingly. Pulitzer Prizewinner, Russell Baker warns, 'The dash SHOUTS. Parentheses whisper. Shout too often, people stop listening; whisper too much, people become suspicious of you.'

colon (:)

The colon says 'wait for it' and 'get ready, there's a load of stuff coming at you'. Either a list, quotation or explanation.

❝ *Her motivation was easily explained: money, sex, love, lust.* **❞** or

❝ *Jerry explains: 'It's boring to sit at home watching soap operas and doing the dishes.'* **❞**

But note that with a normal quote, use a comma not a colon:

❝ *He says of Kelly, 'She's a gorgeous woman'.* **❞**

quotation marks ("") and ('')

These identify direct speech, and turn an actual term into a virtual one, casting doubt without necessitating comment:

❝ *Walker himself is a little light-headed in his praise of the 'reforms' alleged to have been carried out in the earlier Wilson years.* **❞**

Every publisher and publication will have their own requirements on the use of single or double quotation marks, especially when quotes come inside quotes:

❝ *Cindy explains: "I went down into the kitchen and he said, 'What the hell are you doing here?' before throwing a glass at me."* **❞**

Most provide a style sheet giving directions on this, whether to use quotes around the titles of books or names of ships, and so on. Remember that where a quotation extends over more than one paragraph, each paragraph needs opening quotation marks, but only the last should have closing ones too.

apostrophe (')

This indicates possession:

❝ *Britain's balance of payments deficit.* **❞**

and contractions of verbs in colloquial speech and writing:

❝ *The family's got it all . . .* **❞**

Sub-editors are never keener than when restoring your verbs to their full form because of house style. Since this change can play havoc with the tone of your prose, check when reading the magazine whether contractions are ever used, and if so, whether sparingly or as a matter of course. Some editors require *'80s*, others *80's* or *80s*; some prefer *Dickens' novels* to *Dickens's novels.* . . The more of these decisions you anticipate and get right in your copy, the more efficient you appear and the more work they may offer you.

Never confuse *its* with *it's*!
Its means *belonging to it: It came in its own box.*
It's means *it is: It's a beautiful day.*

question & exclamation marks (?) (!)

Both endings to sentences, but use sparingly. If you use too many exclamation marks (known as screamers!) it loses impact. Only use a question mark when asking a question.

66 *How are you feeling today dear reader? In fear of your life? Your honour? Your safety?* 99

You can ask yourself questions within a piece to further the story and link sentences and themes.

66 *Why is it women are always talking about food and dieting whereas men just eat?* 99

hyphen (-)

Not to be confused with a dash. Hyphenate when a noun is preceded with adjective and adverb compound.

66 *It was a never-to-be-forgotten event.* 99

But *no* hyphen when the compound follows the noun.

66 *The event was never to be forgotten.* 99

It's useful to throw in a complex description:

66 *A guitar! One of those half-witted instruments, like the accordion, that are made for the Learn-to-play-in-eight-days E-Z-Diagram 110–IQ fourteen year olds of Levittown!* 99

Of course this can be overdone.

66 *She cast me one of those Hey-baby-why-don't-you-come-up-and-see-me-sometime looks.* 99

Use a hyphen when noun and adjective precede noun:

66 *A year-long war.* 99

Also with adjective and noun:

66 *A two-day course.* 99

Sentences & Paragraphs

The rhythm of your prose will depend on punctuation, but even more on the length of your sentences and paragraphs.

Sentences can be long or short for differing purposes. Exaggeratedly short sentences are dramatic. Staccato sequences of short sentences can set a scene instantly, without exposition. You can almost hear the voiceover:

Manhattan. Late afternoon. A sudden downpour.

A longer, more descriptive sentence is designed to envelop and enfold the imagination:

66 *As the afternoon drew on, stormclouds crowded the Manhattan skyline until, quite suddenly, it was pouring with rain.* **99**

Short sentences can dramatize feelings too, with an intensity that a longer sentence would distance and dilute:

66 *I was angry. Jealous. Full of hate. The bastard! How could he?* **99**

If you find yourself having problems punctuating a sentence or arranging all its clauses rhythmically, the chances are that the sentence is too long. Chop it up.

66 *During the unprecedented absence of her husband Michael, on an exchange year in France, Anne Foster, commissioned to write the catalogue for a New York exhibition, reluctantly engaged an au pair, for the sake of the children.* **99**

66 *Her husband Michael was away from home for the first time, on an exchange year in France. Anne Foster herself was busy writing the catalogue for a New York exhibition. Reluctantly, for the children's sake, she engaged an au pair.* **99**

Even though in your mind the sense runs on, don't be afraid to let your reader assimilate it piece by piece, with pauses for (mental) breath. Editors and publishers' readers can frequently spot an amateur writer by long, convoluted sentences which show their author is not *listening* properly to the effect he or she is creating.

Paragraphs conventionally demarcate the beginning, development and conclusion of a particular line of thought. New thought, new paragraph. How many sentences are in each depends on how you think; but also on how far you trust your reader to think.

I would suggest that you don't make your paragraphs *too* long because people get bored quickly when asked to read a solid block of text, no matter how interesting the prose. Without any thresholds to overcome, the reader never feels the thrill of getting anywhere. Reaching the end of a paragraph, a page or a chapter is a reward. A pat on the back and a measure of how far he has read. If there were no paragraphs or pages, the reader would soon get fed up and stop reading.

The Art of Presentation

Okay, so you've discovered you can write, you've found your voice, you have something interesting to say and you've said it as well as you can. You've been over it and over it until you're sick of the sight of it (and then, if you're wise, just one more time). It's perfect.

Presentation is where many writers fall down. As with school homework, neatness and tidiness mean everything. It's deeply psychological. The more expensive the paper, the blacker the typewriter ribbon and cleaner the type, the easier it is to read.

Unsolicited manuscripts are frequently submitted on odd sizes of paper, pinned together in the corner, typed on a machine whose ribbon was last changed in 1965 and lavishly encrusted with dried globs of *Tipp-Ex*. That's not to mention the coffee-stains, and the telltale dog-ears and half-flattened creases that show half a dozen other editors have already thumbed through this offering and, obviously, rejected it.

There's nothing that shows up the amateur writer like the obvious effort to save money by cramming words onto paper without leaving margins, single-spacing because that way you use half the number of sheets, and it weighs less at the Post Office. *Don't do it.*

Buy white A4 bond, 60–80g weight. It shouldn't cost you much more than a fiver for 500 sheets. Buy a new typewriter ribbon while you're at it. Buy ten and ask the stationer to give you a 10% discount. You can always use up the fading ones for your own copies, the ones that editors won't see. Buy carbon paper and a pack of A4, 45g weight, for your carbon copies.

Type with double spacing, leaving an inch or more all the way round. This is for the convenience of the subs and copy-editors who will need to scribble things in the margins and between the lines, and for typesetters whose equipment may clasp both the left and right sides of the sheet, thus obscuring anything written too close to the edge. Type on one side of the paper only. Don't fasten pages together with anything more permanent than a paperclip. If your piece is a story or an article of substantial length, preface it with a title page, which should contain only the title, your name and address and an estimate of its word-length.

Leave a deeper space than usual at the top of the first page of the text; then type your title followed by your name. Each following page should have a simple abbreviated title—one or two words—and your name or initials. If you number pages at the top right-hand corner it makes it quicker to rifle through and find a particular page; though some editors' style sheets will direct you to number pages at the bottom in the centre. Courses in journalism will teach you to put 'MF/' (more follows) in the bottom right-hand corner of each page until the last, where you should put 'ENDS'. This is standard practice in America, less crucial here. But if you do need to insert extra copy into already numbered pages, make sure it is clear what it is and where it goes. For complete clarity and safety, you should also indicate that it is coming up and that it has just happened—like this:

```
                                   155 (follows 154B)

                       154B (follows 154A
                              155 follows)

               154A (follows 154
                      154B follows)

       154 (154A/B follow)
```

Tedious and complicated stuff, but now if any one page of your insert goes astray, its absence will be noticed.

Always keep copies.

Any manuscript up to about five or six pages should be folded *once*, in half, and posted in an A5 envelope. Anything thicker should be sent unfolded in a full-size A4 envelope. Mark your name and address clearly on the back of the envelope. Better yet, deliver it by hand.

And, unless it's been commissioned, *always* include return postage, and preferably an s.a.e.

All the expenses—materials, typing, photocopying, postage—can be offset against income tax if you're self-employed.

Machines and the Writer

By the time you read this book, this section will undoubtedly be out of date. Electronic typewriters and word processors become obsolete in the space of a couple of months.

Nevertheless, this means that there is a fair chance of picking up something desirable and not very old second hand.

the typewriter

This book was roughed-out on a Smith Corona electric typewriter with interchangeable ribbons and correcting ribbon. Except for the times when I felt really lazy when I sat on my leather couch with my feet up using a Canon electronic portable Typestar 6, which has the advantage of being incredibly light and silent.

Then, when I'd roughed everything out I used a CPT 5425 word processor and single-feed daisy-wheel printer to edit on and top-copy out on. The word processor has changed my life and I cannot recommend it highly enough. Put it this way—if I could marry it I would. The snag is, when you're just starting out, (a) you haven't got the money and (b) you don't yet know whether you will be using it as regularly as you hope.

Nobody gives a longhand manuscript a second glance. Whatever you use initially you will need to get it typed, either by a friend or by a professional typist, who won't be cheap. Current estimates are between £1–£2.50 per thousand words, so for a 60,000 word manuscript we're talking anywhere between £60–£150.

And many typists (whether they have spanking new golfballs or not) make a lot of mistakes in 60,000 words. So a good typewriter and an ability to type is essential. Preferably electric, although a portable manual will do—as long as it has a new ribbon!

The best advice is to spend as much money as you can on a good electric typewriter with a correcting ribbon and then, when you start making a decent living, you can get a portable—for those times when you want to disappear to Malta for a month to work on the book; and eventually, when you start making more than just a living, get a word processor.

There are several new 'electronic typewriters' around like my Canon Typestar 6, which has a display screen where you can check what you've written before it prints it. Brother make two similar models but their keyboard is not as nice. All will memorize a page of text which is useful. They are quiet machines which cuts out complaints from the neighbours at 4.00 am when you're tight on a deadline. And they are incredibly lightweight. I've even typed a piece while in the passenger seat of a car. These machines use a thermal printer and are very good except for a few things. Firstly, you tend to forget when you've got to the end of the page and it's really annoying when you think you're motoring through lines of copy and the printer is just going over and over the same line and secondly, their range of functions is limited, in that they can't underline and type at the same time.

the word processor

Word processors are merely typewriters with a screen instead of paper and a memory stored on a disc instead of more paper. The advantages of a word processor are:

- It is an efficient and clean method of storing and retrieving words. They stay where you file them and don't get lost or forgotten.
- You can change the order of words, sentences, paragraphs, pages or chapters without slicing your manuscript into bits and pasting bits over the top with squiggly lines to show what goes where. While you're playing around on the screen, your original version is still there safely on the disc. If you decide you don't like the new version better, you can change it straight back at the touch of a key.
- Editing is painless. You can insert new material at any point, and the machine will invisibly mend the text, and even justify the margins if you tell it to. Some word processors enable you to juggle a huge range of typefaces, sizes, italics and bold type at will.
- You don't have to print anything until it's absolutely finished. But you can print interim rough copies.
- You can make as many copies as you like, each perfect and identical (though it may still be cheaper and will certainly be quicker to print one and photocopy it).
- While it is printing, you can do something else: make a cup of coffee, go to the loo, or even, on some machines, get on with the next bit of writing or editing.

Disadvantages of the word processor are:

- The continual need to instruct the machine to save the work you've just done on the screen; and the advisability of copying each disc you need onto a back-up disc. Discs are not indestructible, whatever advertisers claim.
- Power cuts and hiccoughs in voltage can erase your work from the screen, though not usually from the disc.
- The v.d.u. can cause eyestrain and headaches.
- Printers falter and break down with annoying frequency.
- They are still expensive things to buy. It's especially important to spend a lot on your printer.

The good news is, of course, that as the technology improves and proliferates, prices tumble. The phenomenon of 1985 was the Amstrad PCW 8256, priced at £399 (plus v.a.t.)—less than many electric typewriters. The price included all the hardware—an inoffensive green screen, a keyboard designed for word-processing, and an integrated printer with automatic single-sheet loading and tractor feed for continuous stationery, and a choice of printing facilities: high speed or high quality. I bought one, and have been recommending it to everyone ever since.

❝ Do be wary of the dot-matrix printer. The printed image, made up of dots, is imprecise, generally too light, and very hard to read. More and more readers, including myself, are refusing to read them. **❞**

PETER DAY, *publisher's reader*

Who Writes on What?

Rumer Godden, author of *Thursday's Children*, advocates writing in longhand and gives the most sensible reasons for doing so. 'People write too fast. I think a typewriter runs away with you. It's valuable to have to pause and search for a word, and writing in longhand slows you up.'

Julie Burchill, Jackie Collins and Jack Higgins wouldn't be seen dead anywhere near a word processor. Julie Burchill types everything on an Olivetti—'a big one'—while Jackie Collins and Jack Higgins both scribble in longhand into foolscap notepads. Jackie has a secretary type up her manuscript once a week while Jack does it himself.

Jeffrey Archer has never been able to type and is notorious for scribbling down his writing in longhand, using a blue Tempo felt-tip pen and Mars Staedtler HB pencils on Oxford foolscap pads—he won't use anything else. His secretary then types it onto a word processor, after which Jeffrey feels comfortable editing on screen.

Frederick Forsyth is a typewriter man and Colleen McCullough a typewriter woman, both preferring to compose straight onto typewriters—the latest Silver Reed and 'anything' respectively—while Arthur Hailey and Len Deighton fully embrace the new technology and compose straight onto word processors.

Len Deighton says, 'I use an Olivetti dedicated word processor, which does fancy things,' while Arthur Hailey gets positively sick if he goes for longer than a week away from his IBM display writer: 'I love that machine!'

John Irving, author of *The World According to Garp*, is happy with his old IBM electric typewriter. 'It took me a while to get used to the electricity of it. I adjusted from a manual typewriter very slowly. I had to turn the motor off in between sentences because it was such a distraction. Now I find I'm so dependent on the motor that when I have nothing to write I just sit there and turn the motor on.'

Tom Sharpe has *fourteen* typewriters, and uses the nearest one to hand. And who lies on her couch with a dictaphone, for her secretary to type up later? Barbara Cartland.

WRITERS' PROTECTION
Writers' Organizations

The National Union of Journalists

The NUJ is an active and crusading union—so I understand. I've paid them a fortune in subscriptions over the years, and they've never done anything for me. The union's answer to this would be that their work benefits all journalists; that we'd be getting paid even less if it weren't for their negotiating power; and that therefore all journalists should join.

The National Union of Journalists
314 Gray's Inn Road
London WC1
(01) 278 7916

Anyone who earns at least 70% of their income from journalism is eligible to join. Membership costs £104 a year; or you can apply to pay 1% of the year's income. There's a temporary membership of £20 for those just starting out, and it goes down to £2 if you're still a student.

The Writers' Guild of Great Britain

The Writers' Guild is also a trade union, affiliated to the TUC. It was founded in 1959 as the Screenwriters' Guild, and still maintains a particular concern with writers for TV and film. It provides a minimum terms agreement and is always negotiating to get more publishers to agree to sign it; a similar agreement is in operation with the BBC and commercial television. It publishes a monthly newsletter and has a full-time staff to give advice on business and legal questions; it will take up cases over contracts whose fulfilment is in dispute. Membership is open to anyone who has had a full-length work, or an agreed number of shorter works, published, broadcast, performed or exhibited. The annual subscription is 1% of your previous year's income before tax, from a minimum of £30 to a maximum of £480.

The Writers' Guild
430 Edgware Road
London W2 1EH
(01) 723 8074

The Society of Authors

The Society of Authors was founded in 1884. It's a trade union, and tends to be regarded by the pushy, campaigning Writers' Guild as rather a genteel organization—an image that is being shaken off. Apart from union representation and negotiation, however, the benefits it offers are broadly similar: business and legal advice, including pursuit of complaints; information about agents and publishers; BUPA, retirement and emergency benefit payments; membership of special interest groups; a quarterly journal and other publications. The Society administrates a number of awards. Eligibility conditions are also much the same: full membership for those who have a full-length work published

The Society of Authors
84 Drayton Gardens
London SW10 9SB
(01) 373 6642

in the UK (not at their own expense) or 'an established reputation in another medium'; associate membership for those who have minor or occasional works published, broadcast, etc., or a full-length work sold but not yet published. Both cost £50 a year, or £45 by direct debit.

Literary Agents

If you're writing books, get an agent as soon as you can. Unless your first book is obviously going to be a commercial success, you may well find it difficult to get anyone to take it on before you've placed it with an agent. But—even though it may rankle to give away 10% of the deal you've negotiated yourself—there's a very strong case for going immediately to an agent and letting her or him sort out the contract for you. Robert Elms says: 'I have an agent for books only because I don't understand contracts and I would say yes to anything they offered me. I'd rather have somebody telling me if it's a good deal or not for 15%.'

An agent's job falls into three parts: support and guidance with what you're writing while you're actually writing it; selling your writing; and 'after-sales service'—including working out contracts, dealing with other rights, chasing publishers for payments due, and generally building on the original sale.

A good agent is one who errs on the side of optimism, who admires your work and counts as a friend, and who has numerous contacts and pursues them aggressively and effectively. It's unlikely you'll find one this good straightaway, if ever. But remember that an agent's primary instinct and interest should be commercial. He or she must push and exploit your ability in ways you wouldn't or couldn't do alone. An agent should not consider you unless your writing shows promise and potential, and you show a compulsion to follow through a good idea and develop it successfully. A book or story submitted by a reputable agent will get quicker and closer attention from a publisher than any other submission. One submitted by an agent who's considered a bit of a joke will have a hard time being taken seriously, however good it may be. From an editor's viewpoint, agents exist to pre-select writing that's worth further consideration.

When choosing an agent, do shop around. Look for one who works for a reputable firm, has respected clients, and has knowledge and contacts in your area.

It always seems to the novice that an agent is doing them a big favour by taking them on, especially when the prospect of earning good money is remote. But remember: your agent works for you, not the other way around. If they don't seem to be doing well for you, go elsewhere.

Authors love to moan about agents

66 I don't think one agent ever took the book out of its envelope. He came to see me and said the reason why he hadn't sold it was because I hadn't revised the manuscript in time. Since there hadn't *been* a revised manuscript, I thought it was a bit irregular. **99**

DYAN SHELDON, author of *Victim of Love* and *Dreams of an Average Man*, and former commissioning editor

66 One of my previous agents never encouraged me. The only time she took me out to lunch—the *only* time—she spent the whole time being excited about selling the film rights to her husband's novel. And the last thing you want to hear is how well your agent is doing for somebody else. **99**

EMMA DALLY, author of *Surrogate Mother: One Woman's Story*

Just as some authors hate all publishers on principle, some clearly believe that agents are parasitic middlemen, and that the whole business would run much more smoothly without them. But, as Pamela Buckmaster of the Carnell Agency points out: 'Publishing is the only business where one party signs a contract at the advice of the other party. You simply *have* to have an agent to get any semblance of fair dealing.'

Agents Talking

Ed Victor, of the Ed Victor Agency, Pamela Todd from A.P. Watt and Felicity Bryan of Curtis Brown are three very respected agents with a good deal of expertise. Having interviewed each of them separately, I thought how interesting it would be to imagine them all gathered around one table for a symposium on the business of literary agency.

How did the literary agent first come into being?

Pamela Todd:
We are the oldest. A.P. Watt started in 1875, with Rudyard Kipling. The notion of the literary agent didn't exist until Alexander Pollock Watt, a solicitor and friend of Kipling's, began looking over his contracts. A.P. Watt thought there was a business in it and approached other writers.

Ed Victor:
It has changed, though. Agents act much more as editors used to act. I think many more agents have taken on the front line editorial role; very often I'm involved in

deciding what will be the next book, should we do this, should we do that; and very often books are shown to me at a very early stage.

Felicity Bryan:
Another important development is the tremendous movement between the editorial staff of publishing houses these days. There's such an enormous amount of change that your average author is unlikely to keep up with events and is likely to be a victim of them, too. He needs a professional whose main job is to keep up with changes and who can advise him on the best place to go.

EV: Authors flit much more from publisher to publisher because commissioning editors move around so much, but authors don't flit from agent to agent. Philip Roth told me he had moved three times with an editor but when the editor moved a fourth time, he stayed put. 'I decided to get off the train,' he said. Big time authors are much more apt to find a stable, calm centre with an agent than they are with a publisher.

FB: Also, the author needs to get on with his writing. We see our function as looking after authors, not just for books, but for any kind of writing. We have a very large TV department, and if they are interested in that, we can help. If they want to write for foreign markets, we can help there too.

PT: There are many more people involved and we're not just talking about publishers. There are newspapers, magazines, film and television rights and many other different rights.

FB: Agents are much more creative these days.

EV: That's right, copyright is infinitely divisible and you can cut it anyway you want. There's a cut called British rights, there's a cut called American rights, a cut called Canadian rights and then there are endless possibilities: film, TV, cassette, cable, and software ... the most lucrative deal I've made in the last two years is one for Douglas Adams for a computer game of *The Hitch-hiker's Guide to The Galaxy*. It's sold over 200,000 units at about $40 a shot.

PT: The whole purpose of having an agent is to have somebody to represent you. A publisher could represent you but an agent offers a much more personal service and is in a position to exploit opportunities that the publisher can't be bothered with. What we do is take one piece of work and get as much out of it as possible. Every single first novel doesn't make *Book At Bedtime*, or is made into a Nicolas Roeg film, but at least the options are there.

EV: All these media areas need what I represent, namely creative talent writing in English. In the beginning is the word. Always. Every movie starts from a screenplay and so on ... There will always be work for those people. And agents dominate the Anglo-Saxon publishing world.

FB: There is also the other element, that writers are quite lonely people and the agent is also a friend, an advisor and somebody who can keep them in touch with the outside world. I think it's crucial that the writer gets on with the agent. Some agents manage to represent writers who they really don't like at all, and that's very professional; but I couldn't work with somebody I don't get on with.

PT: The role of a friend works well when the writer is embarrassed to approach a publisher with an idea. He can often talk it over with an agent more easily. That's why the agent has to respect and quite like their author.

FB: We get thousands of manuscripts sent in. What we find is that authors get an agent when their manuscript has been turned down; and when you look at the publishers that are turning them down you find that they've contacted the most inappropriate people.

PT: One is always looking for authors. I still try to have that excitement of opening a new manuscript whether I've asked for it or not. It just might be a Ken Kesey or a James Joyce, but I have to say, it is a disillusioning task because there is a lot of dross. And there's nothing you can say to that author—all right, it's perfectly well written and we could probably get it published, but so what? Vetting manuscripts is an unpaid side of the job.

FB: Sometimes we do seek out authors. Not so much for fiction. Occasionally if we see a lovely short story we may write to someone. It's more with non-fiction: say, somebody wants a biography writing.

PT: We have people coming to us all the time, asking, What have you got? What's good for a film?—new things as well as old things ... like *The Wicked Lady*, which we'd all completely forgotten about. It was lying quietly on the shelf and the next minute it was a film starring Faye Dunaway. Often TV and film buy off the peg. They come to us and say, 'What have you got with a black lead and a red-headed heroine?' or they want a romance or a crime thriller. And the job of an agent is not only knowing the people in the business, but knowing which of those people wants what and is hungry for what.

EV: Agenting can be very rewarding. One of the pleasures of being an agent is seeing everything first. It's wonderful when something unheralded flops on your desk and you pick it up and know it's a winner; and you put your judgement and reputation behind it. Another thing is successfully managing an interesting career. You have to be constantly thinking about strategy—I mean if somebody writes a terrific book, you have to sit back and really think about the best thing to do with it. Do I sell it in America first, or Britain? What about TV rights? Or merchandising? Finally, I would be lying if I didn't tell you that it's a great kick to sit down and talk about millions of dollars. When people in the book business sit down and talk about seven figures, it gets exciting!

Agents & the Journalist

There are agencies like the *Solo Syndication and Literary Agency* (8 Bouverie Street, London EC4Y 8BB, (01) 583 9372) that maintain a stable of writers on a miscellany of subjects, more or less in a vacuum. The writer produces an article, and the agency sends it out to any magazines to which it might be even marginally relevant. This seems all wrong to me. Because the pieces are written with no specific magazine in mind, their style and content are so generalized as to be useless to any particular one. By the time topical pieces or interviews have been even part of the way around the circuit they are invariably out of date. For all these reasons, agency work always needs rewriting to suit the style of any magazine which accepts it. This means a reduced fee for the writer, reduced further by the agency's cut. What's more, writers are inhibited from reaching their full creative potential by wasting time and energy writing for a market which is indeterminate and therefore wholly unresearched.

Having been on the receiving end of this kind of pre-fabricated journalism, I must say that to an editor it seems quite insulting.

For magazines and newspapers, unless you are a complete agoraphobic or entirely bereft of basic social skills, I would forget about agents altogether. Meeting your editors face to face allows you to get to know them, and get to know what they want. You can build up relationships that are more than just financially rewarding, and further them by following an editor from magazine to magazine. Why let an agent have all the fun? Or all the lunches?

The only agents who can really be of any use to the journalist are those with excellent contacts abroad. After selling First British Serial Rights to a British publication, you are at liberty to sell the same piece over and over again.

How to Sell Yourself

preparing your portfolio

As soon as you start getting work into print, you must start to compile your cuttings book or portfolio, for the edification of future employers. I've always used a clear plastic A4 folder with about 100 pages (available from good office stationers). I always preface each article with the cover of the issue in which it appeared. This helps someone leafing through to remember whether or not they saw that issue.

Put your most recent work at front and back. Be selective: fillers get in the way. Too thick a portfolio will immediately seem dull and laborious. Put some thought into how best to display the variety of your writing. It may be better to have several thin portfolios, each highlighting a different style, topic or area you've worked in.

A loose-leaf portfolio is essential for the freedom to reorganize and update, and to tailor your presentation to the sort of publication you're approaching. If you're selling interviews, fill it with interviews. Be flexible.

business cards

The art departments of most magazines have whole walls full of brilliantly creative business cards from illustrators, photographers, designers and make-up artists. Editorial departments do not feature similar displays. Writers are the slowest of media professionals to learn the art of selling themselves.

Not being graphically minded, many writers never get around to providing themselves with a business card at all.

Do get a professional to design it for you. You may be able to strike a deal with an illustrator or graphic artist by allowing her or him to incorporate a design credit into the artwork of the card in return for a discount. It may not sound like much of a deal, but point out that you will be sending your card to hundreds of editors, and it will be advertising her or his work as well as yours.

I did my first card myself with Letraset, and a girlfriend did the photo-mechanical transfer for me. It cost about £12 for 250 from Prontaprint. My next card was done by Panos, the Deputy Art Editor on *Company* magazine. I'd interviewed Boy George for *Cosmopolitan*, and his picture had appeared on the cover: the first time a man had ever had that honour. The media buzz attendant on that was all good publicity for my interview. To make it even better, some paparazzo in Paris took a picture of George, sitting in the back of a limousine, reading the *Cosmo* interview. Being a firm believer in the maxim, *If you've got it, flaunt it*, I had the picture put on my business card. Now people I give it to at once say: 'Oh, did you do *that*?' As usual, everyone remembers the star, the cover and the magazine, but nobody ever remembers the writer.

It's a good principle not to put too much on your card. Keep it simple. Expand in a covering letter. On the card itself, clever design apart, name, address, phone number and what you are (WRITER) will say more about you than American Express ever will.

publicity photos

A good portfolio, a smart business card and a striking publicity photo all help project information about you into the competitive world of freelance writing, and protect you against being forgotten when you're not around. Everyone remembers a good photo, and the name that goes with it.

Pseudonyms

It's handy to have another name up your sleeve. You might want to write regularly for one publication under one name, and for a second, occasionally, under another. Or you may find a magazine has a policy of not admitting that two articles in one issue are both by the same person.

A pseudonym is useful when:

- You want to experiment with writing in a different style or different area from usual. Usually the incentive is financial. Novelists who write slowly and whose books sell only modestly well will often take the chance of paying the rent by doing a quick bit of novelization, text for a movie tie-in picturebook, or something more sleazy. Rarely do they want this work considered as a significant part of their career.
- Your real name doesn't fit the image of the market. Bestselling romantic novelist Vanessa Royall is really history teacher and ex-US marine Michael T. Hinkemeyer. ('I read *Gone With the Wind* and *Forever Amber* to get the hang of it,' he says, shyly.)
- Researching areas where it would be embarrassing or dangerous for your real name to pop up: undercover interviews, features on drugs or gun-running; or less sensationally, when investigating dating agencies.
- Trying to get round an editor's blind spot. Science fiction writer Robert Silverberg, faced with rejection by an editor he suspected of anti-semitism, resubmitted the same story under the staunchly Protestant name of Calvin M. Knox, and sold it at once. Remember you'll need to come up with a second address too.
- You want to avoid expectations that have built up around your work, especially in your own mind. When I'm writing under my pseudonym Andrew French, I feel different, and write much more aggressively than when I'm Paul Kerton. Doris Lessing pulled a fast one on the literary world when she submitted a new novel, *The Diary of a Good Neighbour*, as the work of Jane Somers. Both her regular publishers rejected it firmly. Curiously, the publisher who did buy it was Michael Joseph, who had published Lessing's first novel in 1950.

'As Jane Somers I wrote in ways that Doris Lessing could not.'

DORIS LESSING

PAYMENT

66 The thing about being a writer is, I'm always
scared that somebody's going to catch on. One day
there'll be a knock at the door, and it'll be a little
man with a bowler hat and a briefcase, and he'll say:
'I'm sorry, you can't do this. You can't actually get
paid for writing.' Then I'll still write, but I'll have to
get a real job as well. 99

NEIL GAIMAN, *freelance writer and interviewer*

Sometimes it seems that between writers and editors the
subject of payment is delicate, almost embarrassing, and to
be mentioned as little as possible. In almost every other
profession the purchaser asks the providers of the service
how much they charge. A plumber doesn't fit your new sink
and then say, 'How much are you going to give me?'

For some reason, very few freelance journalists broach the
subject of fees at a briefing or initial discussion of a piece of
work. It may be a hangover from the painful sensitivity of
the unpaid, amateur writer, who asks no more than to see his
or her name in print. To have your words set out in type,
printed on glossy paper and disseminated among hundreds
and thousands of readers feels like a reward in itself. To be
paid for this honour is almost superfluous, quite beside the
point. To complain that payment is inadequate would be
boorish, not to mention risky.

Editors, who obviously have to buy the best they can for as
little as they can manage, can only capitalize on this
squeamishness. Rates for writing are so flexible between job
and job, and between one writer and another, that to state a
price is almost to invite the writer to begin bargaining.

And so it should be. There are enough uncertainties and
disadvantages in the freelance career without having to
accept bottom rates every time of fear of appearing ungrate-
ful. There's the cashflow problem, for a start. Freelance
journalists are normally paid on publication. 'On', of course,
here means 'not before': you'll soon learn how long it takes
the financial machinery of the proprietors of your particular
magazine to cough up a cheque. One month, two, even three
months later is quite common. Sometimes you can hurry it
up by making a fuss; often, you'll only be wasting your time
and effort. This time-lag means that you could very easily
start the groundwork for an article before Christmas, write
and deliver it in January, see it in print by the end of March,
and not get paid until the summer. And that's working for a
monthly. If it's a quarterly, the delay can be even worse.

This cashflow problem may need explaining to your bank manager. If there's a communication breakdown, you may find yourself having to change to a bank that is familiar with writers and the press. Try Fleet Street branches.

There are no absolute or even standard rates for freelance journalism. The NUJ set down guidelines, shrewdly assessing the wealth of a broad variety of publications by their income from advertising.

Magazines

The NUJ has freelance agreements with some of the big magazine groups (such as IPC and Morgan Grampian). However, since these agreements cover a wide range of publications, the minimum rates can be exceeded on most of them.

There are thousands of magazines, ranging from a dozen or so in the super-circulation bracket, through specialist trade and consumer publications, to small minority interest periodicals. It would be impossible to recommend the same rates for all of these, so the NUJ bands the rates according to the prosperity of the publication and its ability to pay.

Circulation alone is not a reliable guide, since many controlled-circulation professional magazines and newspapers have small readerships but, because of their advertising revenue, can pay relatively well for material they buy.

Magazines are therefore banded broadly according to advertising rates, which reflect their prosperity. The NUJ can provide information on the magazines within each advertising band and the recommended rates for writing, research, sub-editing and design.

NUJ rates have no legal force. You have no justification in expecting them if you're not an NUJ member; and if you are, the only way you can be sure of them is by refusing to work for less. You'll almost certainly find you can't afford to turn down work that pays a mere fraction of NUJ rates. Your best bet is to be (a) reliable, so that the work will keep coming in, with rises in pay once they start to rely on you; and (b) flexible, so that you can take advantage of any and all opportunities, rising swiftly to the demands of the higher-paying markets.

I once left London and went back to Yorkshire for a while, to try to write a novel. To keep my journalistic hand in, when the words weren't flowing, I rattled off a letter to *Yorkshire Life*, explaining who I was and what I'd written for, and suggesting an idea for an article, a tongue-in-cheek appraisal of Yorkshire women. The editor liked the idea, and called me to his tiny office in Otley. I asked about money.

His rate was £15 per thousand words.

A thousand words is a thousand words, whether you're writing for *Smash Hits* or the *Tatler*, the *Barking & Dagenham Post* or the *Financial Times*. I'd have put the same time and energy into the piece, whoever it was for. From my point of view, it would have been jolly to have a piece in *Yorkshire Life* and its cover in my portfolio, but what on earth was the point of writing a thousand words for £15 when I could write a thousand words and sell them elsewhere for £200?

Well, of course, there are other considerations. You have to spread your work around in order to get known, and to begin to attract editors who will pay extra to get not just copy but *your* copy.

66 There are some magazines like *Face* and *Harpers & Queen* which don't necessarily pay an awful lot, but which are a tremendous showcase for your writing. The trade-off of financial reward versus larger recognition is considerable, because the differences in pay for the same effort and creativity, depending where you sell it, are unbelievable. 99

PETER YORK, *writer on style*

You may have a particular commitment to a certain magazine, or a certain range of subjects, which will keep you working on a particular low-to-middling level with hardly a glimpse of the richer rewards gleaned by the more competitive or compliant. You may have prior demands on your time and abilities (*that* novel) which prevent you from aiming single-mindedly at the big money. And then there's a kind of compassion: most top freelances have one or two 'charity' outlets where they regularly write for well below what they are worth—for the hell of it; for a cause; to help a mate out; or out of fondness and gratitude to a publication or editor who helped launch their careers.

In his first year as a writer, Keith Waterhouse made £2. The next, he earned nothing; the third, £12. Hunger is a strong spur on the drive for recognition. Meanwhile, if you're starving, check your rights. 'There may be bad times', says arts writer Abigail Frost. 'It is possible to get social security as a freelance. However, if you are signing on, you can get into trouble over declaring or not declaring income, as the people in your local benefit office may not know the regulations for irregular earnings or even understand the principle. You're supposed to tell them if your income changes by more than 50p a week. A freelance's income changes by more than 50p *every* week! You have to provide accounts, or at least keep records and work out an average per week over three months. There are few accountants who can cope with anybody who's been on and off unemployment or supplementary benefit. The best are those who deal with actors who are often out of work, then often earning huge sums.'

Payment for Authors

Because authors you hear about in the media tend to be Jeffrey Archer, Sally Beauman with her $1m advance for *Destiny*, or Clare Francis advertising American Express, it's a popular myth that all authors are rich and famous. It's not true. Geoffrey Wheatcroft reflects on his book *The Randlords*:

> 66 From when I began to think seriously about the book until when it was at last delivered had been four years. Knocking off time for journalism, and fun and games, it is reasonable to say that I had devoted two years' work to the book. It had earned me less than £6,000, and £3,000 a year is not a lot to live on! 99

Writing books is not cost-effective. Each book is a gamble, for the author as well as the publisher: an investment in the hope of reprints, sales of foreign rights, deals with film and TV producers. All these rights, rates, terms and conditions of payment are contained in the *contract*.

Despite the long and dedicated efforts of the Writers' Guild and the Society of Authors in getting publishers to sign their Minimum Terms Agreement, there is no such thing as a 'standard contract'. Fiction agent Pamela Buckmaster says: 'A contract isn't a formality. It's a record of an agreement between two parties. As such, it's *always* negotiable.' Even if you can't get your advance raised, you can sort out all the clauses to your mutual convenience.

Here are some of the major points to watch for:

Work schedule
This specifies the length of the manuscript and delivery date. Make sure the publisher makes a similar commitment to publish the book within a specified period—usually one year, rarely more than two.

Payment
Certain sectors of the book industry will require you to accept a single flat fee: books written for packagers, for example, or introductions to coffee-table books. Otherwise, your royalty will be a percentage of the cover price, and you will be given an advance against those royalties.

Advance
Usually this will be paid in three stages: on signature of the contract; on delivery of the manuscript; on publication.

It's obviously in the publisher's interest to make the first payment the smallest and the third the largest; and it's equally probable you may want to get these proportions reversed. Short of parting with all the money before you've written a word, publishers are usually willing to be flexible.

However it's staggered, always hold out for as large an advance as possible. Don't be afraid to ask for more than they offer at first. Your advance is all you have, pending legal hearings and settlements, if the firm goes bankrupt in the meantime, or is bought up and 'reorganized'. Correspondingly, if you've sold the book on the strength of a portion and outline, penalties may be payable if you don't deliver, or if what you deliver isn't up to standard. Most publishers are aware that getting back what they've already paid you is about as likely as world peace, so probably will prefer to write it off against tax; but if there's still money owing to you, they may well deduct from it the cost of getting someone else to rewrite your book.

Royalties

These vary in units of $2\frac{1}{2}$% according to what sort of book it is, how much the publisher has invested in it, how large the print run will be, who you are and how many other books you've written, etc. The royalty on an ordinary hardback novel is normally 10%; on a paperback, $7\frac{1}{2}$%. Illustrations, especially colour illustrations and photos, will mean the book costs more to produce, and the author will get a lower royalty. A clause called something such as 'Presentation of accounts' will tell you how often you receive royalty statements and cheques; usually yearly or half-yearly.

Rights

Your publisher will keep a fat slice of whatever they can get for whatever rights you sell them, and pass the rest on to you. As well as British and Commonwealth rights, there are American and Canadian rights, world rights, rights for translation into a foreign language, TV/film/video rights, merchandising rights (which can be very lucrative if yours is the sort of book you can name a yogurt after) and serial rights (for extracts in magazines or newspapers, which make wonderful publicity for the book itself). The tendency is for publishers to sell all these to the highest bidder, which may not be good for your reputation. Signing the contract means accepting that their decision on such things will be final; but the better your relationship with your publisher, the more you can expect to be consulted about any deal. If you reckon you or your agent could do better selling the book in America, say, the answer is to withhold the US rights.

Reversion of rights

Insist on a clause which allows you to get the rights back within a certain period after the book goes out of print and the publisher shows no sign of reprinting.

Responsibilities of the author
Is there a clause that makes you responsible for seeking permissions for quotations? Paying for illustrations out of your own pocket? Indexing the book or paying an indexer? Updating the book at yearly intervals for no extra payment? Make sure you know whatever extra work you're incurring.

Sub-contracting
It can happen that a publisher who has second thoughts about a book, or gets into financial difficulties before publishing it, can sub-contract or re-sell it to another publisher without the author's consent and any further payment or negotiation. Beware of these secret escape routes.

Remaindering
Remaindering occurs when a book isn't selling well and is deemed to be taking up expensive warehouse space. Large quantities are suddenly sold off at huge discounts to 'bargain bookshops' or mail order dealers. This is perfectly common practice, and quite legitimate. What you must do is ensure there's a clause in the contract requiring: (a) that the book won't be remaindered until a specified period has elapsed (the A.P. Watt Agency contract states two years); (b) that you, the author, will be informed of any decision to remainder and offered first refusal on any books about to be disposed of.

Option
Because your publisher is not only investing in your book but also in you, there's sure to be a clause requiring you to give them the first option on your next book (it may be wise to amend that to read 'next similar book'). Though this has led to some notorious pieces of unpleasantness in more rarified regions where publishers are prepared to fight for 'possession' of a prize author, in the beginning this may be to your advantage: at least one door is already open for your next manuscript. Make sure that the wording doesn't prevent you from publishing a similar sort of book elsewhere if they should turn it down. And then get working on it.

Public Lending Right

After years of campaigns, committees and consultations, the PLR scheme was finally inaugurated in 1982, to make token payments to authors, editors and illustrators whose works have been borrowed from public libraries. New provisions came into force in January 1985.

• read
The PLR Act 1979
(HMSO 30p)
The PLR Scheme 1982
(HMSO £2.95)
Amending orders SI
1847 (HMSO £1.30)

• write to
The Registration
Supervisor
Public Lending Right
Scheme
Bayheath House
Prince Regent Street
Stockton-on-Tees
Cleveland TS18 1DF

To be eligible you must be resident in the UK or West Germany, and author (alone or with no more than two other authors, illustrators, etc listed on the title page) of a published work which has been offered for sale. If this is you, send off for your PLR form today. It includes space for personal details and a list of eligible books, their publishers, dates, ISBNs, etc, and requires a statutory declaration, witnessed by an MP, lawyer, doctor, Minister of Religion, etc. Those books then remain on the register forever; new books can be added at any time by filling out a new form and making another statutory declaration.

What you get is a share of a lump sum allotted to the scheme each year by the government. Your portion (£5,000 maximum) is based on the number of times your titles have been borrowed from a sample of twenty libraries. These figures are multiplied and adjusted to arrive at a statistically probable result. With your first PLR payment you receive a remarkably clear description of the process; in fact all the information sent out by the PLR Registry is surprisingly straightforward and comprehensible, given the size, complexity and bureaucratic nature of the scheme.

Enterprise Allowances

'There is a great discovery still to be made in Literature, that of paying literary men by the quantity they do not write.'

If you've been unemployed for at least three months, and have not been self-employed as a writer for at least a year, you can try your luck at applying for a Business Enterprise Allowance—details from your local Jobcentre. It pays you £40 a week for a year while you get started.

The significant hurdle is that rule about not having been a writer already: a Catch-22 if ever there was one. 'No one would seriously consider going freelance without some sort of track record and without some evidence of previous sales they're unlikely to consider you for a grant anyway.' If you've sold only a couple of things, and can persuade your interviewer that these were done not as a job but as a hobby, earnings from them can be discounted. Remember, 'Enterprise Office staff find the regulations as irksome as you do . . . and their own jobs depend on handing out allowances to as many people as possible.'

The emphasis of your application must be on your commercial nous, *not* your creative genius. 'Waffling about novels and Art is a waste of their time and yours; they know you can earn more from a couple of articles in the right magazines than a first novel in hardback, and if they don't they want you to tell them. It's better to seem overly cynical than a daydreaming dilettante.'

I'm quoting freelance writer Alex Stewart, who wrote up the story of how he got his Enterprise Allowance and sold it to the *New Statesman* (17 January 1986). Now *there's* enterprise for you.

Accounts and Tax

Freelances pay National Insurance at the self-employed rate. The best way to handle this is by direct debit from your bank account (unless you can trust yourself to trot down to the Post Office and buy your stamp every week, even when the cashflow is down to a trickle). The DHSS will give you the necessary leaflets NI.41 (*National Insurance Guide for the Self-Employed*) and NI.208 (*Contribution Rates*).

Freelances are similarly liable for income tax under Schedule D for the self-employed. Just because you don't wear a uniform or clock on and off at regular hours, don't assume you're invisible to the Inland Revenue. Far from it. The largely self-regulating nature of our declarations of earnings can bring us under close and suspicious scrutiny. The trick of managing good relations with the IR is to take the initiative. Call them up and ask for guidance. Your local district inspector's office can be very helpful if you show yourself to be open, honest and co-operative.

The very best thing you can do for yourself is to get an accountant, someone already familiar with writers and their circumstances, who will already know the routines involved and the savings to be made. In America everyone files their own tax return, and on the whole they seem to cope with it very well. The British system is not designed to be operated by the individual member of the public. A qualified accountant will be respected by the IR, will talk their language, and can use this professional standing to your advantage. She or he will cost you money, but will save you time and anxiety, and should, after a while, begin to be able to save you more than her or his own fees cost.

Your accountant will require copies of your bank statements (generally there's no need to open a separate business account), the pay statements you receive with your cheques, and receipts for your expenses.

Allowable expenses really can mount up. The financial year ending 31 March 1987 is the last during which you can claim 25% capital allowance on the price of 'plant and machinery' bought for your business—i.e. typewriters, tape recorders, word processors, etc. The expenditure does not have to be necessary, merely 'wholly and exclusively' for business purposes. If the IR decide there is 'duality of purpose'—that the item is also for private or leisure use—the claim will be disallowed.

By the same token, you can't claim for food, drink or clothing, even when you've bought smart new clothes and

Read
● *Starting in Business*
(Inland Revenue booklet
IR28)
● *Money Which—Tax
Saving Guide*
(published annually in
March by the
Consumers' Association)

taken an influential editor out to lunch. The IR reason you've got to eat and dress anyway. But you can claim for everything you use to prepare your work (stationery, typewriter ribbons, notebooks); for research materials (books and periodicals, including daily papers); for typists' fees, photocopying and printing; for postage, travel for business, and a modest proportion of rent, heating and lighting bills; and for subscriptions to professional organizations, and even agents' and accountants' fees.

Get receipts; file them in chronological order; note payments received and expenses incurred in two columns in a little pocket diary. Let your accountant do the rest. Make sure you're reasonably prompt with your accounts each year, as the IR have a quick and easy way of dealing with people who aren't. They simply issue an estimated assessment. Unlike gas and electricity bills estimated according to the season, the weather and your normal consumption, estimated tax assessments are hugely inflated, showing vastly more than you could ever earn or owe. The onus is on you to file your appeal within thirty days, and then prove what the real figures are. Overdue tax is charged interest at 8%.

If you're fortunate enough to win a literary prize of some kind, and the IR try to tax it as part of your income, you may be successful in appealing with reference to the 1979 decision of a Special Commission that Andrew Boyle's 1974 Whitbread Award should not be taxable. If conditions are comparable, precedents like that count greatly in your favour.

WRITERS' PROBLEMS

Common Ailments

being misunderstood

Only other writers understand what a writer's life is all about. Everybody else—parents, relatives, lovers, spouses and especially friends—is liable to think it's easy. They always will until they actually try to write something. Because so much of the work is invisible—going on inside your head, often while you're apparently doing something else, or just staring out of the window— other people tend to assume that it's automatic, a 'gift'. Because they can't tell when you're working (just as *you* often can't tell when you're working), they think you're not, or that it's not important. They will barge into the room and put a record on ('Oh, you're only writing'); they will telephone you and chat for hours; they will bully and cajole you until you give in and go out to the pub with them. It's because writing is so solitary, so self-centred and self-determined, that we are vulnerable to these calls to sociability.

writer's block

This is the most famous affliction of writers, experienced by all of us, though it can hit different people in different ways. Some writers, previously perfectly fluent, suddenly find themselves with nothing whatsoever to say—no ideas, no images, nothing. Professionals caught like this in mid-career sometimes turn to menial work (writing 'novelizations' of popular TV series, for instance) to keep their hand in while waiting for the stimulus to return. Working journalists shouldn't find it too much of a problem to get some more routine commissions for a while. Beginners might try writing long and detailed letters to all those friends you haven't seen for ages, explaining how you simply can't get started writing anything, and how terrifying it is ...

More problematic is the sensation that you know what you want to say, but it just won't come out: a sort of mental constipation. Sometimes it's best just to pack up and go for a walk, or see a movie. Maybe it's time for a holiday— something else writers can miss out on by not having 'regular' employment.

autonomous finger syndrome

This occurs rarely, but can be very distressing. You know exactly what you have to write. The resource material, facts, figures and quotes are all at your fingertips. The tone and style don't pose any particular difficulties. But for some reason, what you have in mind gets lost somewhere on the way down, and you find yourself writing something completely different. It's as if your fingers are just doing what they want. From a pragmatic point of view, and certainly from the point of view of the editor waiting for your copy, this is just a malfunction. But from a Freudian point of view, you should definitely pay close attention to whatever it is that you didn't expect to be doing! That's the area of authentic creativity. Systems musician and video artist Brian Eno has 'Honour your mistakes' as one of his cardinal principles.

submission paranoia

Sometimes it seems that the worst part of the process is handing work in. The spectre of school homework rises from an inky grave. You've spent days getting it done and now it's going to pass completely out of your control into the hands of someone you've no control over, someone who's going to judge it by criteria that are completely inscrutable to you, someone who's going to say whether or not it's *right*. Will they like it? If they don't, how will you cope? Is their judgment to be trusted?

rejection

In freelance writing everyone has to face rejection. In the beginning the disappointment of getting a rejection slip can be quite intense. Take heart: it gets less so as you go on. And the only remedy *is* to go on.

There's a terrible temptation to look at your first rejection slip and think, Oh, well, I suppose my piece wasn't good enough for publication after all; when in fact, all you're justified in concluding is, my piece wasn't good enough for *this* publication. Try elsewhere. Or try again with something else. Read and re-read the magazine you are approaching. Are you sure you have a good working sense of its tone, its angle, its personality? (Because you can be sure every one of the writers who contributed to the issue you're reading does have exactly that.) Was your piece properly targeted?

The same is true of books and publishers. Every publisher is continually inundated with unsolicited manuscripts, of which 80–90% get rejected, often because they're just not up to standard, but equally often, because they're just the wrong *kind* of books. Get a catalogue of your target publisher's books for the next six months (ring the publicity department and ask politely). Read it carefully. What's right for one firm will be wrong for another, *for that reason*. Publishers, like any manufacturers, compete to stay in business, which means finding an area of the market and making it their own—not copying what another firm is doing. Is your book really a proposition for a smart, shiny, impressive hardback, or would it be better as a cheap and cheerful paperback? Even within the same firm, hardback and paperback divisions can have totally different approaches to what they publish and how.

Check all these things first, and then you won't be wasting a publisher's time and conjuring up false hopes in yourself where none exist.

It's important to remember that rejection is not personal, it's professional. Editors are not rejecting *you*, just whatever it is you happen to have written. And it may be that it's only this particular subject that's unsuitable, or unsuitable just at the moment. If so, they'll usually let you know, especially by the fourth or fifth attempt.

Once you've begun to sell material, you may be able to find yourself an agent. Meanwhile, console yourself by thinking of all the famous books that were rejected time and time again before finally finding a publisher: *The Lord of the Rings*; *Watership Down*; *All Creatures Great and Small* . . .

acceptance

Having something accepted for publication may not sound like much of a problem, but there are two reactions to beware. One is to assume it's just a piece of luck, like a prize in a lottery. It's not luck. It's a professional achievement. The work you did was suitable, and up to standard. That editor will be glad to see more work from you. Editors *want* writers who will become regular contributors. You have someone's attention: don't let it lapse.

The other problem is to assume that all your worries are over! One acceptance doesn't guarantee anything, let alone make you rich and famous. You can spend a cheque ten times over before it finally arrives, two months later.

Small Ad Seduction

During those long periods of depression that set in when the rejection slips are piling up and your prize manuscript is getting dog-eared and disillusionment chips away at even the most optimistic of spirits, that's when the small ads catch your eye with that friendly, hand-on-the-shoulder cheer-up-we-know-how-it-feels type of sentiment.

Tempting headlines like 'If you have written a book that deserves to be published write to . . .' or 'Your book published and marketed' can scramble your thinking when you are at a low ebb. But no matter how low and depressed you are or how many publishers have turned down your manuscript *don't* ever be seduced by the small ads.

Don't even think about subsidy publishing. There is only one test of a good, well-written and commercial book and that is whether or not an established publisher will publish the book at no cost to the author.

If you have written a good book then a publisher will pay you money for the privilege of publishing it. If you have to pay to have it published then this probably means that your book is not up to standard, or perhaps not quite what the market demands at that time.

If this is the case, this is something you have to be terribly grown-up about. Just about everybody I know who writes has at least one aborted project lying on the shelf.

the bestseller that never was

I once went back home to Yorkshire to write a novel which I had set in my mind and for which I had tentative approval if not full-blown interest from a publisher. Basically two unemployed guys with brains decide that if they can't earn money then they will have to steal money. But rather than steal from just anybody, they will steal money from criminals who have already stolen the money. Therefore they retain their nice guy images (Butch and Sundance?). They aren't really doing wrong by stealing from crooks, and the crooks obviously can't go to the police and report the robbery of stolen money. Consequently they rob the robbers and live happily ever after.

So I went home to write this opus with everything (plot, characterization, dialogue) set in my head but for some reason unbeknown to me, instead of writing what I should have been writing, I ended up writing a book about a Japanese peasant boy who comes to England and ends up fighting for Britain in the Second World War.

The story was absolutely ludicrous, and embarrasses me even now. Not surprisingly, the book encountered plenty of hostility. Even my agent couldn't say anything more enthusiastic than: 'I think it would have a very difficult time getting published in the present market.' I had to face up to the fact that it was not going to be a runaway bestseller. Indeed, it would never be published at all.

You can only write these experiences off *as* experience. No matter how disappointing, even painful, it is to throw your lovingly-nurtured manuscript in the bin, or leave it on the shelf.

But that is what you have to do. Many a writer fails many times before winning through to print. During these low spots, vanity publishing seems to be a lifeline.

Don't succumb to vanity publishing. You will lose money, respect and motivation. You will gain nothing.

Here is what they actually have to offer.

Stockwell_____

Stockwell's catalogue reveals a good deal with titles like *Seen*

the Hounds? ('a very humorous book based on the endearing characters aboard HMS Malaya and HMS Calypso')
and *Diary of a School-Marm* ('a humorous portrayal of life
as a school-marm in the difficult years during World War
II'). Vanity publishers prey on people who regard their lives
as interesting and (often) comic, but lack the skill to turn
their experiences into anything other people can appreciate.

Stockwell will not quote their charges for publishing a
book until they've seen the manuscript, but will print 'one
contribution' of 28 printed lines of poetry in a 'well produced' book with 'an attractive case binding and gold
lettering' for £21, which entitles you to three copies of the
book itself. Will anyone but the contributors ever see a copy,
let alone read one? If this is good enough for you, why not
submit your work to one of the many, many 'little magazines' and pamphlet anthologies of poetry produced by
individuals and groups all over the country? They won't pay,
but they certainly won't charge you for the service. As for
that amusing autobiographical novel: you might care to sit
down and work out how much it's likely to cost you, at £21
or even at £15 for 28 printed lines.

Merlin Books

'War memoirs, autobiographies and poetry' again . . . Merlin
Books are based in Devon. Their directors are Derek and
Barbara Stockwell. Merlin won't divulge any charges either,
though they do entice you with the prospect of reviews.
'Copies of the book are sent to a selection of journals to
review prior to publication, although we can give no under-
taking that reviews will in fact be printed.' Which journals
and how many? Well, none you've ever heard of, for a start,
as literary editors even on the flimsiest local rag would never
connive at vanity publications, let alone support and ap-
prove the practice by giving them any publicity.

Merlin are even better on the subject of the initial print-
run. 'We undertake to produce whatever number of copies
may be demanded by the sales.' And, since bookshops won't
stock them and nobody ever buys them, that could well turn
out to mean they're not obliged to print any. But they will.
You'll get your three complimentary copies.

The Book Guild

The Book Guild are at least forthcoming about their
charges. 'It has been calculated in the trade that a publisher is
committed to an expenditure in the region of £7,500 to
launch a book of average size.' Not, you note, the clearest of
statements as to how much the Book Guild routinely spend.
'Since we share the launching costs, you need take only half
this sum into consideration.' Such generosity! So, the services of the Book Guild will cost you £3,750 to hire. What do
you get for it?

'We will play our part in terms of publishing skills, general administration, seeing the book through all the diverse stages of production, promotion,' etc. etc.

Uh-huh. So you pay the Book Guild to keep their organization in business. How do they make any money? Certainly not by selling books (look in any bookshop). They make their money out of *you*.

Anchor Publications

Anchor's free pamphlet is called *Advice to the Author in Search of a Publisher*, and contains many encouraging stories of great literary figures who actually paid their way into print: Jane Austen, Elizabeth Barrett Browning, George Bernard Shaw, Edgar Wallace, and, everybody's favourite example, Beatrix Potter: *The Tale of Peter Rabbit* was rejected by everyone she sent it to. Eventually she paid for her work to be printed herself.' Nowadays Beatrix Potter books and spin-offs are an industry in themselves. But what Anchor omit to mention is that these writers did not have the benefit of conditions today, when publishing *is* an industry, not a gentleman's profession requiring a modicum of wealth and leisure from *anyone* proposing to practise it. Vanity publishers are preserving the iniquities of the past, when reading was a privilege and there was no call to extend a print run into the thousands.

Copyright

In the UK copyright exists as soon as a work is created in material form. There is no formal method of registration. Copyright lasts for the author's lifetime plus fifty years.

Copyright is designed to prevent the copying of a work, whether it is literature, drama, music, art, film or sound broadcasts. The actual idea cannot be protected by copyright. What is protected is the actual wording or interpretation of the idea. The Society of Authors produce a helpful *Quick Guide to Copyright* (free to members, £1 to non-members).

Copying rights generally refer now to the ubiquitous photocopier, and are frequently the subject of intricate litigation, always recorded in minute detail in *Publishing News* and *The Bookseller*. The 1956 Copyright Act states that a 'substantial part' of a work must be copied before infringement occurs. This in itself was nebulous enough to make for plenty of legal argument, but the whole issue was raised to another plane when, as Stuart Patrick records in *Law for Journalists*: 'The judge in an otherwise unmemorable copyright action made the penetrating observation: "anything worth copying is worth protecting".' As the technology of textual reproduction grows more sophisticated, the struggle for legal definition grows more intense.

The clause of 'Fair Dealing' allows writers to quote portions of works in copyright, without the owner's consent, provided that the quotation is used for the purpose of criticism or review. Publishers' legal departments will have exact guidelines about this, not least because the onus is often on the publisher to seek necessary permissions to quote. The Publishers' Association and the Society of Authors deem that 'Fair Dealing' should permit a quotation of a single extract up to 400 words of prose, or a series of extracts to a total of 800 words. However, beware of quoting all or most of a very short work as this can be judged breach of copyright.

Plagiarism

'Immature poets imitate, mature poets steal, bad poets deface what they take and good poets make it into something better, or at least different.' I lifted this from an article in the *Guardian* by Richard Boston, who nicked it from T. S. Eliot's essay on what Massinger took from Shakespeare. When it comes to imitating, stealing, borrowing and wholesale pillaging, writers are the experts. We all do it, particularly in journalism, where the re-use of quotations is standard practice, and many magazines would be stuck with embarrassing blank pages if they weren't occasionally prepared to run whole articles cobbled together out of quotes from cuttings files.

Fiction is full of unacknowledged debts (for example F. Scott Fitzgerald stole from Zelda).

The more you read and write, the more you absorb into your memory. You find yourself repeating phrases without realizing you've used them before; sometimes it wasn't you who used them. Certain words and phrases—Peter York's *Sloane Rangers*, Joseph Heller's *Catch-22*—are eagerly snatched up and passed into general currency. I claim to be the first person ever to use the word *bachelorette* instead of the ugly and outmoded *spinster*. There's a great pleasure in seeing your own phrase echoed by another writer—and so it's possible to get away with re-using a lot of existing phraseology without formal acknowledgement, though a casual reference to your source, even if it was in conversation and untraceable, does no harm at all.

Libel

Libel is defined as 'a statement concerning any person which exposes him to hatred, ridicule or contempt, or which causes him to be shunned or avoided, or which has a tendency to injure him in his office, profession or trade.' (Fraser on Libel & Slander, 7th edition). To be libel, the defamation must be expressed in permanent form, which includes cartoon, broadcasts and even photos; and 'any person', of course, includes 'any company or group of people'—more on this in a minute.

When suing for libel the plaintiff can sue writer, publisher, distributor, or all three, but in practice always sues the one with the most money, which is usually the publisher. Libel actions, according to Charles Wintour, editor of the old London *Evening News*, 'take up a lot of time; they can cost very substantial amounts of money, and if successful they can only harm the reputation of the newspaper.' The BBC programme *That's Life* was taken to court by Dr Sydney Gee, and ended up paying him £75,000 plus legal costs of 'around a million pounds'. Which is why most libel actions are settled out of court.

In a rather uncharitable piece for *Over 21* magazine, looking at the fashionability of worthiness, and called 'Good Causes for Concern', I mentioned 'Animal Aid, who will even risk blowing up humans to protect their furry friends.'

I was wrong. It was libel.

Animal Aid are a peaceful campaign group who have never done anything more defiant than picket a butcher's shop.

The organization I meant was the Animal Liberation Front, who are reputed to be more militant. I'd even written 'Animal Liberationists' on my rough copy. All I can conclude is that the name 'Animal Aid' must have popped into my head at the crucial moment. I once did an interview with Judy Geeson, an active member of Animal Aid—perhaps that was where I'd (mis)remembered it from. The fact was, I'd made a mistake. A big one.

Over 21 agreed to publish not only my apology, but also a spread for a feature written by the Animal Aid campaign group. Everyone was happy. This is the usual way of settling a libel action out of court. I'd incurred *Over 21* giving away about £5,000 of free advertising—reasonable compensation, and peanuts compared to what the damage might have been.

The moral is: Be careful, be honest, and be accurate.

A highly recommended guide to libel and other legal issues for the freelance is Stuart Patrick's *Law for Journalists* available from:
Media Law Tutors
25 Pine Ridge Road
Burghfield Common
Reading RG7 3NB

MAGAZINE WRITING

Whereas authors of books often work in complete isolation, and don't get paid until years later, freelance journalists have a regular (or at least frequent) source of income, and are very much in the swim of things. Journalism, from *Computer Weekly* to *Cosmopolitan*, from *Books and Bookmen* to *Health and Efficiency*, is the spreading of information, and information is news: new developments/products/theories/releases/scandals/triumphs/disasters. In some areas, journalism is fiercely competitive; in others, thoroughly co-operative. It always is, or can be, remarkably social, with press conferences, previews, launches and lunches giving everyone the chance to congregate and talk shop, swop favours, offer tips, pick brains. As a freelance journalist, you are part of a *network*, and nowhere more so than inside the publications for which you work. The better you understand your place and role in the system, the more you'll be able to contribute to and draw from it.

Inside Magazines

putting an issue together

The place of advertising. The first thing to understand about magazines and newspapers is that one of the main points of the exercise is to sell as much advertising space as possible. With few exceptions (mostly highly specialized journals depending on a dedicated number of readers), magazines owe their existence to the income from advertising.

Most monthly glossies work on a ratio of sixty pages of editorial copy to forty pages of advertising. During the run-up to Christmas, when people are spending more money and looking for things to spend it on, there are plenty of adverts and magazines are thicker than normal. By contrast, in January and February, when the Christmas spree is over, advertising is limited and issues are markedly thinner. In 1985, the January issue of *Harpers & Queen* had 146 pages, the November issue 386. After Christmas, the next *boom issue* is in March, when advertisers feel safe that you, the consumer, have got your money sorted out and are prepared to spend. This is why publishers will always launch a magazine in October or March; never in January or July.

So, even if you despise advertising and pride yourself on your resistance to it, remember that as a freelance journalist, you depend on advertising executives for your living. The more ads they sell, the more editorial pages there will be and the more writing the editor will need to commission.

Advertising also provides a wealth of information about the readers it's aimed at. Simply leafing through a magazine looking at the ads for once, instead of the features, you can get a pretty good idea of who the readers are and who they'd *like* to be: what they're concerned with, what possessions they aspire to, how they use their leisure time, and so on. But more than that, since advertising is designed and placed only after extensive market research, it's the business of a magazine's advertising department to know precisely who their typical readers are and keep detailed files on them, showing how old they are, how much money they've got, where they went on their last holiday, what they eat and where.... It's odd the number of editors and writers who are reluctant to capitalize on this store of information, as if it were somehow 'cheating'. Unlike the advertisers whose favour they need to win, they prefer to ignore research and work on some kind of intuition.

When I'm considering breaking into a new publication, the first thing I do is to read it thoroughly. The next is to call up its advertising department and ask them to send me a *media pack*. Advertising reps are desperate to sell space and will respond to any polite inquiry with alacrity. Within 48 hours a media pack will arrive. It will include: a recent copy of the magazine; an advertising rate-card; a statement of the philosophy of the magazine; and an analysis of its readership in demographic and geographical groups by age, profession and class. Apart from anything else, it's fascinating.

filling the pages

Once the approximate size of a particular issue is determined, the editor and his or her team (Features Editor, News Editor, Associate or Deputy Editors *et al*) hold an *Ideas Meeting*: to decide how best to fill the pages with a good balance of imaginative, interesting, topical, controversial and lively copy.

Regular features. These are the first thing to be dealt with—the music column, the film column, the sport column, the gardening column, the horoscopes. These more or less take care of themselves, being written by regular columnists and usually appearing in the same spot every issue. There is work here for you, if you can corner a particular area and make it your own. Write to the editor, enclosing a piece in a compatible style, tailored to the right length. Arrange a meeting, at which you can make a good show of the appropriate parts of your portfolio. You probably won't be accepted; but you will be remembered, your name firmly linked with your specialist topic. Try again next year; and in the meanwhile, you could do worse than conduct a public debate with the regular columnist via the letters page.

Special features. The special features it includes, and the way it treats and varies them, are what gives a magazine its special identity, the character with which the reader identifies. Here much careful planning goes on. As well as articles on obvious themes like sex, fashion and beauty and working women, a magazine such as *Cosmopolitan* will normally carry three general articles, one major and two minor 'personality' pieces, two or three on emotional and/or medical topics, humour, travel, self-help and occasionally a religious or parapsychological item.

commissioning articles

Once the editors have decided what they should have in the issue, they then have to decide who, from their accumulated stable of staff and freelance writers, should write what. Whatever the ideal line-up, it will have to conform to their budget; and as often as not, the most famous or best qualified writer they'd like is out of the country or having a baby or simply already overburdened with work. A good substitute must be found. This is also an opportunity for you, as an ambitious new writer; the catch being that *as* a new writer, even if *you're* on your way out of the country or having a baby or already overburdened with work, *you can't say no.* Opportunities accepted tend to breed more opportunities in a way that opportunities rejected rarely do.

The writer is called in for briefing, or briefed by phone (more on this on p. 72), and given a deadline.

planning the layout

The writers have all said yes, the features are commissioned. The editor sets about making up a *flat plan*, which is a plan of the pagination of the magazine. The ads are put in first; then the editor has to decide where to put each feature, whether at the front (commonly a very busy, bitty section bringing the reader up to date), in the middle (the meaty, most serious features) or at the back (the regular, unspectacular stuff, plus the odd surprise). Illustrations and photographs are chosen to complement each piece.

This stage is hectic because things keep changing right up until the last minute. While you are busy researching and writing your article, your editor is re-thinking the length of articles and the balance of the issue. If a competing magazine comes out with a four-page special on something that's just been commissioned, that idea must be scrapped and he or she must move on to something else immediately. Other ideas get shelved because something brighter turns up. In 1985 I had an interview with Jackie Collins scheduled for the September *Cosmopolitan*. Then Cher won the Best Actress Award at Cannes for her performance in *Mask*. Out came my Jackie Collins interview; in went a profile of Cher. The Collins interview was rescheduled for November, but by then so many other magazines had interviewed her that the moment was lost and the piece scrapped.

Editors may find they've commissioned two very similar pieces; or two pieces they've commissioned have turned out to be too similar. One will make way for the other.

While the editor is juggling for a balanced issue, the number of editorial pages is fluctuating as more ads are sold or lost. An editor can suddenly be landed with eight more pages—or eight less—than he or she thought.

deadlines

By this time the first copy is arriving. Some of it is brilliant, some better than expected; some worse, some wretched. This will alter decisions too. A nice idea that hasn't quite come off will probably get two pages instead of three, one instead of two. These and dozens of other crucial decisions are invariably made on the spot, while the Art Editor is pressing for a decision on an illustration, three people are holding on three different phones, and the editor is dying to go to the loo. At times like this, the writer's welfare is the last consideration.

in-house work

The Fawlty Genius of John Cleese.
66 A minister of silly walks, a mad hotel owner, an SDP spokesperson. But now for something completely different. 99

PAUL KERTON

When the copy has been scrutinized and re-read by the editors, it is copied for the art department and the sub-editors. The piece is given a *title* and a *strap-line*.

The art department design a layout, perhaps with an illustration. The sub-editors (known as subs) are precision English specialists who check the copy for accuracy, spelling, grammar and punctuation, and make sure it fits both the layout and the *house style* (conventions observed by the magazine on verb contractions, words ending in *ise* or *ize*, etc.). Then layout and copy are sent to the typesetters.

proofs

Proofs will be checked by the subs for errors and last-minute editing or justifying to made the copy fit the space available. Some magazines send some freelance writers proofs too. These must be checked and returned without delay; sometimes editors request writers to phone in any corrections. This is not an opportunity for rewriting, not least because the exact layout is now set, and typesetting is a costly process. It may be that your imperious last sentence has been mangled because a line just had to go. When the proofs are passed, the type is transferred on to film and sent to the printers.

After a further complex journey through wholesalers, distributors and retailers, the magazine is bought by the reader, who generally knows little or nothing about all that has gone before. Your name is on your article, and he will hold you responsible for it in every detail, you, the writer.

lead times

Putting an issue together and getting it out takes a long time. Another thing that the general public hardly realize, but that journalists have to take as a fact of life, is that all publications work well in advance of their actual cover date. As a rule of thumb, monthly magazines work three months in advance, colour supplements and other weeklies work six weeks in advance, and most dailies 24–48 hours in advance. Your deadlines will be based on this, so editors will be best pleased to discuss possible contributions a bit sooner still.

66 Deadlines are little cowards. They do not travel alone. Deadlines go in groups of three or four, and they leap out on you all at once. 99

NEIL GAIMAN, *freelance writer*

Know your editors

There are good editors and, alas, bad editors; helpful editors and frustrating editors; imaginative editors and dull editors. As a roving freelance, you'll need as many strategies as there are editorial types. Here's a preliminary guide.

'If I don't trust an editor, I won't work for them. I won't have anyone I wouldn't trust to perform open-heart surgery on a child working on my copy!'

KIM NEWMAN, *freelance writer and critic*

The Great Editor
Knows exactly what she wants and how to communicate it to you. The brief *will* be brief, concise and to the point. She will remember what she's asked you for and require you to deliver it, not something else. She will pick you to do things you're good at, even things that will teach you something, and will be able to tell you which issue your piece will appear in. If you meet one of these, please let me know.

The Waffler
He knows he wants something about monogamy, or maybe celibacy, but then again.... He won't so much brief you as have a natter with you, hovering around points for and against and taking in the public transport strike and the price of car tyres. At the end of the hour he will say, 'There you go! Can we have it in two weeks' time?'

The Mind Changer
When she briefs you she knows what she wants. You write it just so. And get it back.

What has happened is that in the fortnight you've been off working on it, she's been having lunches and drinks with everybody in the world and has discussed the idea with all of them. Every new opinion she's encountered has changed her perception of it and her sense of how it should be handled. It's such a gradual process that she doesn't notice it taking place, and truly believes that what she asked you for was the idea she has *now*.

Here, the answer is to take clear, concise notes, and let her see you doing it, so that you can show them to her after she's changed her mind. Better still, though I've never quite had the nerve to do it: take in a tape recorder.

The Old Writer

Having an editor who used to be a writer can work for and against you. He's sympathetic to your situation and understands your needs. He is the one who sends a bike over for your copy to save you a journey. He'll phone you or even send you a postcard thanking you for the piece and assuring you it's fine. He'll consult you about illustrations and proofs.

On the other hand, he will always tend to see a piece only as he would have written it. It may be difficult to satisfy him with anything other than a replica of this, which means either cramping your style, or having him rewrite it.

The Flirt

Journalism, even for the glossies, is nowhere near as glamorous and sexy as is dimly supposed by the general public. However, there are editors who get consumed with a great sense of power and sometimes feel that in return for a commission you might like to make a physical contribution to their well-being!

Rule Number One: Never seduce your editor.

The Meddler

There's a man working on one of the Sunday supplements who is notorious for interfering with his writers' copy and generally messing them about; so much so that there's a secret club for disillusioned victims called the 'We-want-2,000-words-by-tomorrow-but-we-probably-won't-use-it' Club.

When you're sure you're faced with one of these, there's only one thing you can do. Go elsewhere.

Editors talking

Anne Billson, books editor, Time Out
'I get so many unsolicited reviews from people who obviously haven't read the magazine. They're too long, for a start; they don't have the house style, or they get the

tone completely wrong. It's better to show what you have had published already, even if it's in small magazines nobody's heard of. You also have to be incredibly persistent.

'Don't ever appear desperate, even if you have no money and haven't eaten for days. Desperation is always very off-putting. You have to project confidence, as though you've got lots of work, even if you haven't. If you need to go somewhere to follow a story, borrow money. Usually editors will pay if you have to take an interviewee to lunch.'

Adele-Marie Cherreson, editor, Look Now
'The standard of writing is the second phase. The first phase when you're looking at a freelance writer is: Does this person know what the magazine is about? A lot of writers are just too lazy to check out the magazine's contents and the names of staff. I'm still getting mail addressed to my predecessor and I've been here two years! It just seems a very simple etiquette to get things right.

'I feel the more mature a magazine becomes, the less writers write in. We're always looking for tomorrow's writers because *Look Now* has always been a good springboard for new talent.

'Editors are always willing to give people opportunities, but they don't give people second opportunities. That's a hard lesson, but it's something I had to learn when I was freelancing for three years. I'm willing to give people as much time as I can. I will stand over them, hold their hand, go through their copy with them—but if they don't rise to that, if they are lazy and give up, then there is always someone else.'

Pat Roberts, editor, Over 21
'We do not take kindly to writers who do not address us by name. This is a high-profile business and the editor's name appears on the masthead of the magazine. Also, we do not take kindly to manuscripts that arrive as photo-copies as this tells us the piece is doing the rounds. And finally, we do not take kindly to writers who send in submissions without an s.a.e. In fact, we don't send them back.

'We do reserve the right to alter copy, but if we are altering anything drastically, then we would inform the writer. Asking somebody to rewrite is not a personal slight. Pieces often need re-jogging when a writer has strayed off the point.

'Spelling is not a sub-editor's job. It is a writer's. On the top sheet the writer should put his name and daytime telephone number. Also, we need a list of contacts for the people or places mentioned in the copy. Little things matter.

'It is very annoying when a writer who has been
published rings up and asks for ten complimentary copies.
We are not here to subsidize a writer's cuttings book.'

Gillian Wilce, literary editor, New Statesman
'It's surprising how many people don't seem to have any
idea of the nature of the paper they're approaching. They
frequently offer lengthy features, when if they'd looked at
a few issues of the *New Statesman* they'd realize I only
have a limited number of columns, which are almost
always entirely full of book reviews. The more sensible
approach is to write a letter saying you're interested in
reviewing for the paper, and explaining briefly what your
areas of interest and expertise are.

'You need to be knowledgeable about your subject;
ideally, to have that kind of quiet authority which doesn't
need to display itself, but gives the editor confidence that
you know what you're talking about. If you do, and you
write clearly and succinctly, and on time, to the right
length, and all those boring things which surprisingly few
people stick to, you've got a good chance of getting work.'

Noëlle Walsh, assistant editor, Good Housekeeping
'Lots of new writers have good ideas and can write a few
lines about an idea, but don't really think it through. They
don't realize that to write a 15–2500-word feature on
something, they need more than just a good idea.

'You have to have a professional approach. Editors
have to think that writers want to write for them because
they like the magazine.

'If a new writer has written a bad piece, most editors
tend to pay them a rejection fee rather than go through it
with them.'

Marcelle D'Argy Smith, features editor, Cosmopolitan
'Sometimes the professional writer is wonderful and
sometimes he is tired. Sometimes you get better stuff from
somebody who is just starting, who is fresh and trying
very hard for you. Which is why you need both because
you can't rely on either.

'It's very hard to maintain a high standard of writing all
the time. Some writers just send something in and think,
Oh, that will do, and to be brutally frank—it won't.
Sometimes very good writers are so hard on themselves
they never hand anything in at all. Then there are those
writers who think, That's good enough, I'm a professional
writer, I've been published; and really they should have
run it through the typewriter once more.'

Valerie Buckle, assistant editor, Hospital Development
'Trade and technical magazines go only to approved
readers. They're subsidized by the advertising, so they

have to be directed at very carefully researched sections of the industry or whatever. Often they're run by very small staffs, so a lot of the work is freelanced out. Our freelances usually have something to do with the industry; although we do have three regular freelances who do nothing but freelance journalism for trade and technical magazines.'

David Barrett, assistant features editor, Computer Weekly
'Breaking into computer trade magazines as a freelance isn't easy. We don't often print news from freelances we don't know and trust already, because there isn't time to go and check the details. And we don't take many articles from people working in the industry, largely because they're not writers. To be a freelance computer journalist you've got to be able to write, and you've got to have the specialist knowledge. You've got to understand how the business world works, and be able to talk to senior government officials, managing directors, civil servants and union leaders. You've also got to be able to understand a very enthusiastic computer programmer who is burbling on about his wonderful new language. Even if you don't understand it, you've still got to be able to write it up!

What Sub-Editors Hate

Most writers have a pet story about their copy being subbed to death, but they're not always innocent of provocation. Sub-editors hate writers who:

'Some sub-editors are good, and some are butchers. I'm not very temperamental. The way I figure it my writing is so good that even if it has been cut to high heaven, it's better than everything else in the paper.'

JULIE BURCHILL, *columnist*

- nonchalantly ignore the word-limits they've been given.
- constantly get facts wrong, especially if they've been commissioned for their expertise.
- make huge corrections on proofs without consideration for line breaks or deadlines.
- fail to give phone numbers or addresses for the people or companies they're writing about, making it doubly difficult to check facts and spellings.
- persistently misspell words, particularly those who spell a word three different ways in the same piece.
- write huge convoluted sentences that are impossible to break up neatly.
- are overprotective of their copy and shriek if there's a comma altered.
- have never subbed and dismiss it as a menial task.

JOURNALISM

Freelancers Talking

Neil Gaiman is an interviewer and reviewer, mainly for men's magazines like *Penthouse* and *Knave*; he also collaborates on humorous articles with Kim Newman, better known as a film reviewer for the *Monthly Film Bulletin* and *City Limits*. Anne Billson manages to sustain a freelance career while also being books editor of *Time Out*.

Why freelance?
Neil Gaiman: You don't become a freelance writer because the money's fabulous, or for security. You become a freelance writer because you have to.
Kim Newman: You've got no choice. I spent two years trying to get a real job, and at the end I thought, Okay, I'll do what I'm doing and make a living at it. And did.
Anne Billson: I was never going to be a writer, except inasmuch as I wanted to have books published; I never considered it as a job at all. I never thought of writing as work to start with. I thought it was fun!

How did you get started?
NG: I knew two American authors I admired were coming over to the UK, so I got out my *Writers' & Artists' Yearbook* and started phoning Books and Features Editors. I started with newspapers and worked my way down. The *Daily Telegraph* said, 'Why don't you try *Penthouse*?' I did an interview for them, and a couple of other interviews with writers which I sold to places like *She* and *Young Observer*. The cheque from *Penthouse* was more than twice as large as the cheques I got from anywhere else, so I stayed with it.
AB: I spent several years trying to make a living as a freelance photographer, and got into writing by accident. I filled in for a friend doing listings on *Event*, and made a lot of contacts. I was never very pushy, but I got a steady stream of reviews and things, which got steadier. It took me about three years before I started to make anything like a living. You have to be prepared to starve.
KN: But you have to anyway, if you're going to be a freelance. I'm mainly a reviewer, but I also write fiction. Fiction doesn't make that much money, but somehow adds a lot to the portfolio. I think it stops you getting bored with writing about other people's stuff: you're writing your own stuff too. Working on an alternative arts magazine gave me a couple of other skills that you might

not think are necessary, like proof-reading, layout and paste-up. If you know a bit of that, it can make it a lot easier to work as a freelance writer.

AB: You also have to have a tremendous amount of resilience—which I haven't! As soon as somebody turns down something I've written, I take it personally. You mustn't take it personally. You have to have confidence in what you write.

What are the drawbacks of freelance writing? _____

KN: It's a very tiring, miserable job, with long hours. You work harder than anybody else you know. What's more, they don't even think you *are* working. For a writer, just sitting around staring into empty air *is* work.

NG: Only deadlines get me going. The only article I've ever been given without a deadline is still not finished.

KN: I can tell you how to beat that. Ignore deadlines. Do the work as soon as you're given it. You spend maybe two days on a job that's needed in two weeks' time. Do it in the first two days, not the last two.

What do you like doing most? _____

NG: Interviews are an incredibly easy way to make money. All you need to do is keep in touch with the various publicity departments, who always have somebody to promote. You talk to him or her, and you sell the result. You can sell it more than once. I've now made £700 plus a book deal off one interview with Douglas Adams, including selling it to the US, then selling the US interview back here.

AB: Interviewing is very hard for me. I'm very shy, and don't like talking to people I don't know. And I don't find that people are necessarily interesting just because they're famous. You have to *make* them interesting.

KN: I only interview people whose work I know, and whom I'm interested in; but I don't interview for a living.

What was your most triumphant moment? _____

KB: When another journalist came up to me and said: 'One of our readers has asked how many books you've written and where he can get them.'

AB: When you can actually turn down work. I still don't like turning it down, even when the pay's terrible.

Robert Elms: The hip young gunslinger of urban life
At university a mate of mine, Steve Dagger, managed Spandau Ballet (I made their name up), and he said, 'Bob, I want you to write a review of the band and take it into the *NME.* You've always said you could write . . .'

To shut him up I wrote the review, in longhand on a piece of exercise book paper, and took it down to the *NME.* I had to have an edge, so I said to the geezer, 'I think your paper's crap,' and I bombarded him with vitriol and then handed him the review. He read it, said it was really good, and he asked me to make it longer. But still didn't ask me to type it.

And they ran it, god bless 'em, and sent me a cheque for £15.75. I've still got it. I did a few things for *NME* but me and the *NME* didn't see eye to eye and *The Face* had just started. I liked it because it liked the things I liked—clothes, music, nightclubs—and I used the same approach as with *NME*, only the opposite: I told them how good I thought it was.

I walked into Nick Logan's office and said 'Hello, I wrote for the *NME* (I didn't know he used to be editor of *NME*) and I think I should be writing for you.' In the office was a picture of Toyah whose designer I knew. I said, 'You shouldn't be writing about Toyah, you should be writing about the girl who designs her clothes.' So it appeared that I had inside knowledge.

I wrote that piece myself and that's the last time I've ever phoned anybody up or gone into an office gunning for work. I've built up a good relationship with several editors now and we get ideas by a process of interaction. Also, I've developed a tag as a style writer—*New Society* called me the *hip young gunslinger of urban sociology*. For me style is shorthand for sociology: what people wear, where they drink—and I love it. I did history at university and as far as I'm concerned style is social history and I'm really a chronicler.

I do love clothes, I'm addicted to nightclubs, I do go to football every week—even away matches. That's my world and because I came from a working-class background—I grew up on a North London council estate and my mum works in Woolworth's—I have inside knowledge of a world that most writers don't know about, since most writers are middle-class, and have no street credibility.

So if the *Sunday Times* wants a piece on football violence, I can get it right, because it's something I've been a part of. I never write about anything I don't like. I wouldn't be able to.

The actual mechanics of writing I find very dull. I still write my first draft in longhand with a biro. I find writing a slog. I can't work unless there are people around me or the TV is on. If I'm alone and there's no sound I go out because I get bored. I love having written.

Everything I get comes from a phone call. Pete Townshend, now commissioning editor at *Faber*, phoned recently wanting to do a book. I'm not finding the book difficult to write, I'm finding it difficult to sit down and make myself write. There isn't a deadline and I always tend to leave everything until the last minute. Also, everything I write is about 2,000 words so I only know 2,000 words. I'm writing 60,000 for the book, and I'm just writing the same 2,000 words over and over again in a different order. Talking about it is better than doing it.

'I'm grateful to *The Face* for starting me off and I think it's one of the best magazines in the world. Though it pays so badly—if I told you what I got for a feature you'd drink it tonight. But that doesn't matter. It's great exposure, and Nick Logan is the most gifted man I've ever met.

My work doesn't get subbed that often because (a) my writing is very complicated and (b) I write on specialist things. I'm quite willing to re-jig things though.

Writing for me is very much about patterns and rhythms and quite often my writing works more in terms of the way you read it than what it actually says. I can make words and phrases sound interesting.

Writing is all about organizing words, thoughts and ideas and knowing how somebody reads them. That's why I'm a Machiavellian writer. I construct things to have an effect, to wind people up, or to make them feel romantic. And they fall for it. I love it.

Julie Burchill: the brat as moralist

Why did you start writing? The usual corny reason I suppose I was good at English at school and that was the only thing I was good at. My parents tell me I used to write stories but that could just be their romantic view of things. I don't remember.

Who did you write for at first? I began to write for the *NME* when I was sixteen. It was an incredibly adventurous time for them because punk was about. They needed somebody very young. I was ideal.

So you got in on the back of punk? Absolutely. The *NME* staff thought teenagers were a figment of society's imagination, because they were so old. If I had not been a teenager, I doubt if I would have got the job. My writing was so dreadful. Awful. Incredibly immature, stupid; it had a complete lack of structure or any sort of formulated thought about anything. It was just completely mindless—the way teenage writing always is.

How did you get onto the Sunday Times? They came to me through *The Face*—I was writing for them from 1980 to 1984. I enjoyed writing for *The Face* because I was allowed to write about what I want.

What do you like writing about best; I'm not sure. I will take anything on so long as I can be a bit funny about it. I like to be funny. I spent the first part of my career being really serious and poker-faced. So I'm making up for lost time. I would like to think that I could laugh at myself, but I wouldn't like to be tested.

Do editors brief you properly or do you just do what you want? I do what I want. Often I wish they would tell you what to do so you wouldn't have to have your own ideas all the time. I need somebody to give me orders.

How do you work? I work very late at night and into the early hours of the morning. I'll start about eight o'clock at night. I just can't work in the day. I get distracted too much.

Do you use a typewriter or word processor? I use an Olivetti typewriter. A very good one. I have never used a word processor and I never would. That's superstition I suppose. I'm a backwoods girl.

Do you ever do interviews? Never. I tried briefly when I was on the *NME* but I was the world's worst interviewer so I was taken off them. Most people are so dull.

Do you ever have any problems with the bank manager? No, I don't. I never have. I have always fallen on my feet.

What are your ambitions as a writer? I don't have any ambition. I just go along and see what comes my way. There isn't a novel burning inside of me. Absolutely not. Never. I will never write a novel.

What about your other books? The collection has sold out. I have three books out this year (1986). One from *Hutchinson*, one from *Michael Joseph* and one from *Virgin*. The *Virgin* one is a film book that I wrote a long time ago for *Proteus* who went bust. Luckily it was never published so I could sell it again. They haven't stitched me up because I have got two advances for it now. The *Hutchinson* one is a collection of unpublished pieces.

Do you find writing a book hard work? Yes, it's really hard work. It's horrible. I'm never going to do another one when I've got these three out. I can't work without a deadline and the deadlines are so far ahead.

Starting Out

Don't try to run before you can walk. Very few writers get into the *Sunday Times* first go. Julie Burchill was writing professionally for seven years before the *Sunday Times* would take her on. Raw talent is not everything. It takes time to gain ability, credibility and style.

Be patient. If you've tried *and* tried, and still been rejected, perhaps you are just not ready yet. Stagger your ambitions and be honest with yourself about your ability and your potential. The beauty of writing is that the more you do, the better you get, so stick at it. There are publications of every degree of literacy and finesse. Match your ability with the quality of the magazine you're aiming at.

It's rare that a magazine will take something straight off the slushpile and say, 'Thank you very much, it's just what we are looking for.' Why? Because it's too sombre for *Punch*, too radical for *Look Now*, too old for *The Face*, too young for *Woman and Home*, too rude for *19*, too prime for *Knave*, too left for the *Spectator*, too right for the *New Statesman*. . . in short, it doesn't hit a target readership and editors get fed up with writers who continue to send in second-rate work. It's well written, it's funny, it's illuminating, but it isn't aimed at one specific publication. Be specific. Know who you are writing for—talk it over with an editor, before you start.

Finding a Market

Isolate a specific area of published writing that appeals to you, or rather, that your writing tends towards. Generally, Sod's Law applies: people will pay you a fortune for writing something you don't want to write, but will turn their noses up at anything you really do want to write.

There are over 1,700 magazines in Britain, ranging from *Playboy* to *Yachting Monthly*, from *Weekend* to *Ambit*, so there should be a niche for you somewhere. Probably the biggest and most lucrative area for freelance writers today is the women's magazine market. The proliferation of magazines for women means that they differ widely in the way they are written, who they are written for, and what they are trying to provide. There are 49 women's magazines on this graph (from *Media World*, October 1985) alone.

MAJOR WOMEN'S MAGAZINES: AUDIENCE PROFILES

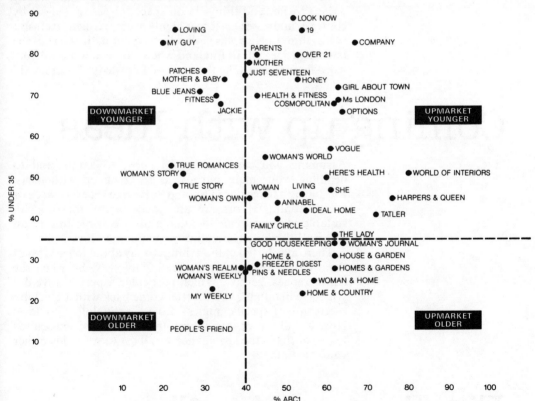

There are magazines for teenyboppers (*Jackie* and *Blue Jeans*); teenagers (*Just Seventeen* and *Mizz*); singles in their 20s (*Company* and *Over 21*); homemakers in their 30s (*Options* and *Good Housekeeping*); the middle-aged (*Woman's Weekly*); and the elderly (*People's Friend*). There are magazines for feminists (*Spare Rib*); women in the arts (*Women's Review*); women in business (*Working Woman*); women with families (*Family Circle*). All offer different opportunities to the freelance.

'We use an enormous amount of freelance writers,' says Pat Roberts, editor of *Over 21*, 'and have the net going all the time. We try and keep a balance between male and female writers, because we don't want the magazine to be written only by women.'

'Most of the people who write for *Look Now*,' says editor Adele-Marie Cherreson, 'are the same age as the readers and write very directly on the same level. The difference is, we have access to a lot more information than the woman on the street and we are sharing that knowledge.'

Eric Bailey, editor of *She*, says: 'We are more outward-looking than most women's magazines. We're not selling or promoting any sort of lifestyle, we're merely reflecting an interest in other people's lives. We use nearly all freelance writers: a hard core of ones we use regularly, and "hobby writers" who send things in on spec. *Harpers & Queen*, by contrast, addresses itself to a highly accomplished, exclusive readership. In Nicholas Coleridge's opinion, 'It is one of the few magazines left in England where you can write a 4,000-word feature, and take the readers' knowledge for granted.'

Coming up with Ideas

Assuming you can write good copy, to length and to deadline, your main purpose is to come up with ideas. Producing a magazine in a competitive market every week or every month, editors are always desperate for original, suitable ideas. *Specific* ideas. It's no use suggesting to an editor: 'I think you should do something on love.'

There may be ten million things to say about love. Most of them have already been covered, copiously. So when the editor replies, gently, 'Which particular aspect of love did you have in mind?', you'd better come back with a quickfire succession of specific angles—Love on the dole; Gay love; How to fall out of love gracefully; Rewards of unrequited love—or that's the last chance you'll get to waste his or her valuable time.

Finding an Angle

From the editor's point of view, the most annoying type of enquiry comes from the person who is going on a trip to or starting work in, say, China.

'Hi. I'm going to China for six months and I wonder if you'd like me to write a piece for you?'

'What sort of piece?'

'Well, a piece, um, on China.'

'What *about* China?'

'Well, I'm not really sure until I get there.'

This is a true test of patience, of which editors generally have more than we give them credit for. They will grimace silently and say, 'Look, go to China, have a marvellous time, write whatever you've got to write and if you think it's suitable for us, send it in and we'll have a look at it.'

Now if you've got insight into the drug traffic inside China, the blossoming of the Beijing fashion industry or Cantonese heavy metal rock, then you've got an angle. An angle is a certain, definable viewpoint, or a look at one isolated aspect of a subject.

The trick is to narrow your focus and concentrate, from one particular angle. An angle is a certain, definable point of view, or a look at one isolated aspect of a subject.

Select your magazine. Identify an area—regional cuisine, Rugby League, nuclear disarmament—that you can be sure they're interested in. Then think of something particular to say about it, with an emphasis on originality: new thoughts, new developments, new experiences, new insight. If you can't think of one, you've chosen the wrong area. Make a few notes.

Then phone your magazine to make sure you're addressing the right editor, and that there's at least a germ of interest (and that there isn't already a piece on Chinese pornography coming up in next month's issue). Then, when after a couple of minutes they inevitably say, 'Put something on paper and we'll talk,' do just that.

The Approach

Write a *brief* letter introducing yourself. Include:

- The name and title of the editor (spell it right!).
- A reference to your phone conversation 'of this afternoon', and what you talked about.
- Something to show you are thoroughly familiar with their magazine.
- A mention of your special qualification to write this piece. (Don't overdo it.)
- A mention of what you've had published in relevant places elsewhere. (Don't overdo this either.)
- Photocopies or tearsheets of a couple of these, no more.
- Outline of some ideas.
- A suggestion of a meeting.

What you are trying to get out of the editor is a commitment—i.e., a commission. The best way of getting this is to meet her or him face to face. It's much easier to wriggle out of commitment in a letter or on the phone. Once you've got an actual editor in front of you, if you don't come away with work you've only yourself to blame.

My initial letters have always been excruciatingly humble, somewhat like this:

---

1 September 1986

1 Shakespeare Villas
Wordsworth Street
Reading
RG9 9ZZ

Honna Blackman
Features Editor
Glam

0734 999999

Dear Honna

I thought the piece on Japanese lingerie in your last issue was excellent and I wonder if I could do any writing for you? I will write anything from serious features to opinion pieces and humour to interviews. Recently I have been published in the Daily Express, Elle, Company and Penthouse.

I work quickly, research thoroughly and always have plenty of ideas. Enclosed are a few ideas that I think might be suitable for your publication. If you are at all interested I would welcome the opportunity of calling in for a quick chat.

Yours sincerely

Paul Kerton

Either attach a separate sheet with your ideas on, or include them in the actual letter. Keep each one brief: you're not writing the feature yet. Don't send more than three of your best ideas to any one publication at a time. Keep a few up your sleeve for the interview. Here are six of mine set out as I would present them.

The Modern Mating Disaster

The cancer of our time is that everybody's looking for Mr or Ms Right and is desperately seeking a partner to settle down with but when that person arrives everybody is scared stupid and does their level best to sabotage the relationship. It's crazy but everybody gets so bored so quickly, dumps their partner and then gets acutely lonely/depressed before grabbing another. Why is it happening and what's it all about?

Quiz: Are You Watching Too Much TV?

A quiz to determine whether or not the reader is a TV slave, a selective viewer or soap opera addict.

Worthiness: Are We All Getting Too Worthy?

What with Band Aid and first aid and flag day after flag day it would seem that we are all getting *too* worthy. But behind the good causes are there any causes for concern? What about those guys who fiddle their charitable expense accounts? And how many outside toilets *really* get built?

Why Successful Women Scare Men Off

I know quite a few women around the 32–33 mark who are attractive, successful in their career, they have a flat, a car (and a cat) and wear great clothes, but despite wanting to develop a decent relationship with a man find that they literally scare men off. Why is it?

Cocaine—The High-Living High-Risk

Already the staple diet of the music and advertising industries, cocaine is the achiever's drug: Yuppie fuel. But contrary to the users' claims, cocaine *is* addictive and the effects of coke-induced paranoia can be horrific. Let's do an industrial on the coke trade from initial euphoria to eventual tragedy.

Men and Violence

There is much outrage about male violence against women but statistics show that the prime target of violence on the London streets is not a single woman but a white, middle-class man in the 25–35 age bracket. I'd like to do a piece about male violence, how it is an inherent part of all of us and how it affects our attitudes and behaviour. Explain what it's like to find yourself in a square-off 'outside' situation and actually get punched in the face (ouch!). Also there's the rush of power you get in an argument when you know you could—if the worst came to the worst—beat the hell out of the other guy.

The Briefing

When you call into the office for a briefing, try not to be too nervous. Smile confidently and make your presence known. Journalists are supposed to show initiative: ask someone where to find your editor.

This initial meeting is your opportunity to size up the editor, just as they are doing to you. To find out what they do and do not want. Some editors are very cranky and have strange prejudices founded upon obscure and illogical pretexts. But if you're aware of these, you can play on them, and get yourself more work. Even if your editor seems the most straightforward person in the world, always have a pen and pad, and write down everything that seems important.

You will need your notes when you get back to the solitude of your room, to remind you what, exactly, it is you have to write. It may have been an idea of yours in the first place, but between you, you and the editor should have outlined the shape and angle it should take. Perhaps it has moved in a different direction from your original suggestion. Did the editor want you to include that item about recent legal complications, or to steer clear of it?

Researching your Topic

Apart from the opinion piece which comes directly off the top of your head, and those pieces that describe personal experiences you've already had, then you have to do research of some kind before you can write anything. Every topic will dictate its own research, whether it involves studying the court transcripts of suffragette trials or finding out the sales figures of Stevie Wonder albums. The only general rule is that whatever it is will take you longer to track down, sift and process than you expect; and that the most fascinating or conclusive details will always be somewhere off at an angle to the direction you're searching in.

Because you're pressed for time, and because you won't be paid for research hours but only for words written, there's a temptation to skimp and skim. Wading through the works of Iris Murdoch to get the exact wording of that elusive quote, or checking the 1929 production figures for the North-East Kent coalfields, would have clinched your argument or turned a middling piece into a brilliant piece. But it meant another day and a half hanging around in the library for a difference of only a word or two. So you scrubbed round it.

There's no remedy or short cut for this. The piece will probably still get accepted; but you know in your heart of hearts how much better it could have been. And when you see a piece of work on an even vaguely similar subject by somebody who did do all their homework, you know how much sharper, more cogent and authoritative it seems.

This is where rejection can actually be a blessing. It stops you getting complacent. It gives you the urgent professional obligation to restore to your work the edge and lustre it had when you first had to prove yourself.

pr agencies and press offices

The purpose of the press office within an organization, and of the PR agency it hires, is to get as much coverage for the organization's product or service as possible, on TV and radio, and in the text of newspapers and magazines. In marketing circles, a glowing mention in the editorial pages of a prestige publication with a large circulation is far superior to any conceivable piece of advertising. It's more persuasive, because the magazine is seen to be endorsing the product ('I haven't laughed so much in years' *Daily Mail*). It's more desirable, because the organization doesn't pay for it; or at least, not directly.

However, PR agencies can be very generous with their clients' money in pursuit of editorial coverage. When Swatch watches were launching a new range, Lynne Franks PR sent all the 'in' journalists and writers a free watch. That may seem extravagant, but it's sound PR. A year later, I'm still wearing mine and thank you very much. Also, I'm mentioning it here.

Just about every product on the market from cars to toilet paper, and from haute couture fashion to farm machinery, is represented by a PR company. If you write in an area of high visibility, as the jargon puts it, once you're established you will be pestered by relevant, and often completely irrelevant, PRs.

Relevant PRs are a godsend. They keep you up to date with the things you'd otherwise have to find out for yourself: new products, new films, celebrities coming to town, etc. If you want to find out more, they're your first source of information.

The *press release* is an announcement from a PR or press office, often so badly written as to defy belief. It's a good idea to get on the mailing list of as many PRs as you can. You never know what information you might need. *Hollis's Press and Publication Annual* is an invaluable paperback directory of all press contacts and PRs.

Rewriting

This begins with a phone call from the editor, saying, 'Thanks very much, love the piece, it's absolutely marvellous—*but...*'

Perhaps you rushed the writing, or had something else on your mind (another couple of deadlines, most likely). Or it may be that your work is fine as far as it goes, but it goes too far, or not far enough. An editor may feel that you're hammering a point (or an opponent) too hard for the diplomatic relations of the publication; or that you've assumed more background knowledge than the average reader is liable to possess.

Whatever. Try not to be too rigid or too precious about your copy. Just because you've been over and over it until it gleams and sparkles doesn't mean that changing one sentence will shatter the patina of perfection. On the other hand, if you're bored with the whole piece, being asked to have one more go isn't necessarily disastrous. A second opinion may be just the fresh thought you need to bring it back to life.

Or part of it, at least. It's very rare that a rewrite will involve overhauling everything from the first word to the last full stop. If a piece is that out of tune, an editor's more likely to spike it altogether (and should pay you a rejection fee, if it was commissioned in the first place). Remember that there are major parts of the writing profession where rewriting is a routine and continual part of the job. Tom Stoppard has been known to write whole sections of dialogue in the dressing room minutes before the curtain rises. It's even more hectic on the film set, where the author can be summoned peremptorily by the director and told: 'You remember the woman written out in scene 3? Well, we've got to keep the actress on, so can you write her back in, please? She's at make-up, so you've got fifteen minutes. While you're at it, we need a completely new death for the old man.' (This actually happened to writer Clive Barker on the filming of *Underworld*.)

There are, of course, times when you will be asked to rewrite something in a way with which you disagree. Well, at least you've been consulted, and not just hacked to pieces. Take the opportunity to discuss it before deciding what you've been asked to do is immoral, dishonest, stupid or even just mistaken. There are some arrogant and insensitive editors around, and letting them interfere with your writing is like lending your record collection to a three-year-old. If an impasse is reached, the only option remaining to you is to pull the piece, and perhaps try to sell it elsewhere. Try to keep the disagreement professional and amicable.

Features

A feature is simply a written piece, usually around 1,500–3,500 words, concentrating on one subject. There are several different kinds of feature, but they all have a similar basic structure. You can begin with what you like (provided it's enticing), end with what you like (provided it's not feeble), and put what you like in the middle (provided it's relevant). What is essential is that there is a single theme running all the way through, sustaining the piece (and the reader's attention); and that the theme must follow a logical or chronological sequence, with each paragraph dovetailing neatly out of the one before and moving the theme along an appreciable amount. Think of the theme as a backbone, with each connection as a strong and snugly-fitting vertebra. Then your feature will be an organic whole.

If you go off at tangents, spend too long on minor points, or hover vaguely around your subject, the theme will be fractured and confused, and the feature will be patchy, difficult to read, and unsatisfying.

The secret of writing a good, tight, satisfying feature is planning. Organize your material so that it follows a very definite line, and passes through a series of crescendoes of interest or conflict. Every writer approaches a feature in a different way; the route he or she takes and the techniques used are as much a part of personal style as the choice of words and the length of sentences. You reveal a good deal about yourself when you write a feature.

Ways of getting *at* material vary from the most passive (watching a movie) to the most active (going hang-gliding by the Pacific). You can interview key people, talk to people in the street, present an official line or make wild unsupported conjectures. Techniques of presenting your material will include description, narration, quotation, recital of fact and expression of personal opinion. The mixture will depend on you, on the subject and the publication, and on the lightness or depth with which the subject is to be treated.

the general feature

Take a controversial topic, a good, juicy one. *War*. A subject of perennial fascination and horror, and one that everyone has a reaction to, particularly around the time SALT talks break down again and international paranoia is running high.

Now we'll plan a feature around it. First give yourself a working title. It may not actually be your eventual title, but it will state your all-important *theme*, so it's worth choosing one under which you might well go into print. Try something provocative, like *If they held a war, would you fight?*

Keep your target magazine in mind, and what the editor said when you suggested the piece. *You* magazine might go for this one—in which case, considering *You*'s predominantly female readership, it might be better to call it *If they held a war, would anybody turn up?*

Writers diverge here. As far as I'm concerned, the big question is: Would the average man in the street roll up his sleeves to defend his country? Have we learned anything from conflicts of the past? What does the prospect of war *now* mean to the individual?

Organize a rough plan on this theme.

1. **Intro.** Another world war isn't too remote a possibility. Design a scenario. Identify a recent piece of international nonsense that could very easily have gone over the brink. Talk to military men, and a politician or social historian known to be particularly vocal about the fear of, say, Russian invasion.

2. **The mood of the nation.** There were lines of volunteers for service in the Falklands war, and high patriotism expressed in unexpected quarters. Would we have the same response to the imminent prospect of (*a*) conflict nearer home, (*b*) nuclear war?

3. **Modern man.** He's incredibly selfish. He enjoys life and is looking forward to a promising future. He isn't keen to get his hair messed up and his £60 loafers shot to pieces.

4. **Modern woman.** Talk to a peace camper. Would she change her mind if she was being raped by a vodka-soaked Muscovite? Talk to a female marine. Talk to a half-dozen school-leavers facing years on the dole. Would they fight? Would they expect to be fought for?

5. **Mistrust of authority.** Argue the case for doubt. We no longer blindly respect our elders, our social institutions, church and government. What is there worth fighting for? *Dying* for?

6. **Doubt: who are you defending?** Contemporary British society incorporates so many races/colours/classes/principles/creeds. Who *are* 'we'?

7. **Doubt: who are you attacking?** Is morale equally shaky on the other side? Is the Russian army really 85% alcoholic? Would they all really defect if they got the chance, in search of a lifestyle of blue jeans and Sony Walkmans?

8. **What would the next war be like?** Interview veterans from World War One and Two, and from Vietnam. Read Michael Herr's *Dispatches*. Extrapolate how the experience of another war might differ. Read General Sir John Hackett's *The Third World War*.

9. **Is anyone really up to it?** We live in an abundance of stories and statistics about the inefficiency of military machines both western and eastern. Pick out a few. A Russian tank can't travel 75 miles without a complete overhaul. SS22 missiles are only 35% accurate.

10. **The able-bodied men.** Talk to them. Would they fight, given all of the above? This should give you some poignant quotes to finish with.

During your research you'll come across people and stories that alter your rough scheme (always in the light of your theme and working title, of course). Perhaps you'll discover that, despite what you set out to argue in points 5–7, we are all actually much more obedient now than we were five years ago, or than we appear to be on the surface in peacetime. This will give your feature new thrust and conviction. Perhaps you'll meet some particularly jingoistic MP, or a female army officer, and use their personality to string the whole thing together. In fact, if you don't discover anything you hadn't set out to look for, you're probably not looking hard enough. Re-design your feature by all means, but keep one theme intact throughout. Check with your editor before making any drastic changes.

the composite feature

This is made up of individual cases brought together on the page for what they have in common: women who have lost babies in 'cot deaths'; teenagers who are making a mint in computers; writers who have married their editors; etc, etc. Work out the common denominator and collect your interviews. Look for the points of contrast. For instance, in a composite feature on abortion, it's good to cover all the angles, whatever your general argument: a couple who are pleased; a couple who are regretful; a couple who split up over it; a couple who didn't go through with it but (if you can get close enough for them to admit it) wish they had.

Composite features are good for getting a lot of variety and colour under one title—say, *Who's working over Christmas*? This is compulsive stuff because it's bound to make readers feel guilty, and people like to feel guilty at Christmas (hence the success of the original Band Aid single 'Feed the World'). At the same time, the guilt sharpens the great sense of relief that, whoever *is* working over Christmas, it's not them. Talk to:

- the Samaritan (inundated with calls from lonely people)
- the Casualty Ward Sister
- the Air Sea Rescue pilot (dropping bales of hay to stranded sheep or picking up the frozen channel-swimmer)
- the hotel worker
- the worthy eccentric (a Famous Name doing something public-spirited on Christmas Day—but not Jimmy Savile or Leslie Crowther again! A Famous Name will always give a feature an extra lift).

the triumph over tragedy feature

Executed to perfection every week in the downmarket women's magazines and institutions like America's *National Enquirer*, where I once saw the headline: *I changed my sex three times in a desperate bid for happiness*. Tabloid standbys include the little girl with polio turned away from six hospitals before a pop star stepped in and whisked her off to a research centre in Houston; the soap opera star who fought back off the bottle; the comedian who went on stage the night his mum and dad died in a coach crash. The world is full of T-O-T stories because tragedy is all around us, indiscriminate in its choice of victim; and because the human being is a problem-solving beast. The will to survive and to survive with some degree of dignity intact is sufficiently powerful for most people to overcome personal tragedy. The mixed appeal of compassion, relief and moral uplift draws in readers of all kinds.

From the reader's point of view, the T-O-T is gripping because it contains RELIEF (Thank God it didn't happen to me) mixed with COMPASSION (Thank God he/she is all right).

There are three stages to a T-O-T story:

1. Describe the quiet domesticity and unhindered normality—the very ordinariness of life, before the tragedy struck.
2. Pile up everything that went wrong and make it colourful. First, how the disaster hit. Next, the side-effects: how her husband deserted her/the kids were taken into care/her hair fell out/the council repossessed the allotment. The works. Lay it on thick and make it virtually impossible for this poor woman to overcome the tragedy.
3. *But* she made it.

the instructive article

The variety of these is so great it's impossible to give general structures or guidelines: How to get a mortgage; How to complain; How to behave when moving in with your lover; How to be a freelance writer. The most difficult thing is getting the tone right, talking from the point of view of experience and achievement to the ignorant enquirer. Avoid being pompous, arrogant or patronizing. And watch the *sequence* of information. Don't slide into technicalities or assume special knowledge: build it up as you go. The only key is to think yourself back to where you were and what you understood before you started whatever it is. Don't be afraid to expose your own past mistakes and misconceptions—in fact, your reader would always rather have that than a slick display of inimitable expertise.

the voyeur feature

The writer as spy. Drop into some activity; choose a vantage point and watch everything that happens; follow somebody around for a day. An afternoon browsing in Soho. A night in an accident ward. On the beat with the river police.

Check that you're not intruding, or in unacceptable danger. Keep a low profile. Make as many notes and tapes as you can without disturbing the natural flow of events. Avoid the people who want to act up for you. Digest everything. Write it up vividly. Include your own thoughts, feelings, reactions; but don't let them get in the way of what's going on. In the voyeur feature more than any other, you are your readers' representative. Tell them what they want to know.

the industrial feature

Not (necessarily) a guided tour round a biscuit factory, but a trade term for the feature that isolates one topic—opera; drugs; market gardening—and explores it in exhaustive detail. Prepare to be obsessed, though preferably temporarily. Afterwards, treat it as a combination of *Instructive* and *Voyeur:*

the opinion piece

Until a publication has established you as 'somebody', with its readers above all, you are unlikely to be asked to sound off in print. Even when you are, there are a few traps to what seems surely one of the quickest and easiest things to write for money.

When I first started writing for women's magazines I succumbed to the temptation of writing what I thought the 'girls' wanted to hear. A mistake. The writing didn't represent my own opinions, but a diluted and consequently unconvincing version. Your readers will soon find you out.

It's better to be honest. You shouldn't get on your soapbox unless you're prepared to get people's backs up: they have their opinions too. Provided your piece is based on sound knowledge, checked facts and statistics, and doesn't stray into libel (see p. 51), then there's no possible comeback you should worry about. There'll be hate mail: 'I must get more hate mail than anybody in the world', claims Julie Burchill, with habitual exaggeration. Julie has made the opinion piece her stock in trade. Her anarchic style, slick turn of phrase, cutting sarcasm and occasional generosity make her riveting reading, even for those who hate her. Two *Time Out* readers had letters about her work printed in the issue for 6 March 1986. One, Jonathan Meres, declared: 'I think that Ms Burchill is absolutely wonderful/crap, depending on what mood I'm in.' Meanwhile on p. 10 Ms Burchill was doing her number, with the volume up full:

66 Every year, like a tired old panto, some group or other appears from the East bearing muscular manifestos and meaningful videos intent on hyping themselves into our hearts, displaying all the respect for human dignity and intelligence of a door-to-door pet rock (very appropriate) salesman. Pop's past is littered with the corpses of the future of rock'n'roll. 99

Interviews

Interviewing is a skill you'll need for research, even if you don't see yourself doing many interview features, and becoming expert at it will help no end with the provision of direct, original and lively material. Depending as it does on timing, alertness and the precarious chemistry of interpersonal communications, interviewing can be tricky, boring and (often) utterly exhausting. But you'll always learn something, and the rewards can be unexpected.

Possible interviewees will be of three types, roughly:

● members of the public with news to tell: the witness, victims, heroes, etc
● experts supplying you with requisite facts or analyses
● celebrities

interviewing methods

Securing the interview is your first task. If you've been commissioned by a publication, credentials will be no problem. If you're assembling material for a book, a little more explanation will be necessary. If you're approaching someone because you reckon they're newsworthy and the copy you get out of them is bound to be saleable, you run the risk of being mistaken for a freeloader, fan or nosy parker—and, of course, of wasting your own time as well as the interviewees because you haven't targeted your work at a specific market and wind up unable to place it.

Some professionals recommend always writing a letter first. If you do this, you should:

● identify yourself (and your publication) briefly
● mention what you intend to ask questions about
● suggest a meeting-place and two or three times and dates
● request confirmation, perhaps by phone

If your deadline's pressing, however, or if the interviewee is only available for a couple of days, this is going to be too slow. It's also easier to turn down a request on paper, when you're not dealing with someone in person or on the phone.

I would recommend always making the approach by phone *through a third party*. Saying: 'Your manager/your press office/a mutual acquaintance (name them) gave me your number' is perfectly courteous enough for any but the most reclusive of respondents (whose number you probably wouldn't get anyway), and shows that you've already been vetted by someone responsible.

Your conversational manner on the phone will introduce your respondent to the kind of interviewer she or he is going to be faced with: brash and talkative young tyro, or urbane old hack. Since you won't be doing interviewing at all if you've got an irritating manner, you shouldn't have any trouble in securing an agreement. If you're empowered by an editor to offer lunch or drinks on expenses, this will help. It's also an important opportunity for your interviewee to make any customary (or eccentric) stipulations, of which you need to be forewarned. Michael Moorcock won't give interviews to girlie magazines. Kenneth Williams would rather no tape recorder (but will succumb to polite pressure).

I was astonished to read in Liz Taylor's *The Writing Business* that she always relies on her memory, never a tape or notes. I wonder how many gems she's lost when a plane went over; how many people feel they've been misquoted by her; if she's ever been sued by one. *Don't rely on memory*.

Unless your shorthand is phenomenal, use a tape recorder. Asking permission first is a courtesy you mustn't overlook, but needn't expect to have refused. The Kenneth Williamses of this world are few indeed. Soul singer Gloria Gaynor gave me my biggest surprise.

'Do you mind if I use a tape?' I asked, putting my Sony on the table.

'Nope,' she replied, 'I think I'll tape it too,' and whipped out a ghetto-blaster the size of a fridge from behind her chair. Morrissey of the Smiths tapes interviews too. It must be something about singers.

Other cautious souls, such as designer Roger Dean, may not want to duel with tape recorders, but will ask to copy your tape. I'd suggest you comply with this, or promise to send them a copy if it's not going to be done on the spot. It's up to you whether you agree to submit a copy of your transcript or your eventual write-up for the respondent's approval. Avoid it if at all possible: it will always mean a delay, and in general interviewees' approved versions are much blander than their original remarks. Better to get them to trust you not to do anything sneaky.

Nicholas Coleridge, five years a columnist for the *Evening Standard* and regular contributor to the *Spectator* and *Harpers & Queen*, observes:

'A plausible manner is terribly important. I find a very good way to open people up is, if they say something that you know is frankly wrong and very prejudiced, instead of jumping on them and saying: "What on earth do you mean?"

it's better to say: "Funnily enough, that's very interesting; not enough has been said about that." Immediately they think you are on their side. Once you are away, they've got nothing on you, unless you've been fool enough to say you'd let them see a proof.'

Nicholas Coleridge, however, doesn't use a tape recorder. 'I'm a notebook man, but I don't use shorthand either. My system is: before I go into an interview I write down a list of about ten areas to talk about. Then, while interviewing, I write in fast longhand, sometimes writing only the first letters of the word. When I've finished, I go through the interview filling in the words from memory.'

I'm not convinced. You can't beat tape for capturing everything without hindering the flow of conversation.

'I like that,' counters Nicholas. 'If you use a tape then you feel obliged to keep the conversation going, whereas when you're writing in a notebook, people expect you to take more time. I always make a point of being amateurish, which seems to relax them. Also, in that space while you are scribbling, people very often add a second sentence or justification of what they were saying.'

But the tape allows you the freedom to respond to what's being said, and *how*. You can pay attention to expression and body-language; and you've got a record not just of the words used, but also of all-important intonations, often subtler than you realize or can recall later. What's more, I often find that writing up an interview involves selecting phrases that didn't seem very important at the time, and that I would not have bothered to write down.

For use I would recommend the Sony TCM7 (about £80) or TCM6 (about £50); or the very solid and reliable TCS-350, which will cost up to £100, but is a stereo model, useful for group discussions around a restaurant table, and, even more important, for entertaining you with soothing or invigorating music on your way to the interview and home again! For telephones, the Sony telephone mike TP-5T, I am told, contravenes certain bugging and invasion of privacy acts, but is damned useful and doesn't cost much more than a fiver. People tend to be more open on the phone. Particularly if they don't know they're being recorded.

Which brings us to the other reason for taping interviews, and for keeping the tapes afterwards. Accusations of mis-quotation can often be calmly turned away by playing back the bit in question. Should legal proceedings ensue, your tape may not be regarded as sufficient evidence, because it might conceivably have been doctored. The Press Council, on the other hand, will recognize tape.

interviewing members of the public

All right, to you they're just useful copy. But to the ordinary person in the street, being interviewed by a journalist, with the prospect of their names and utterances appearing in print, is quite a big deal. They are liable to be flustered, recalcitrant, or else self-important or silly. Nervous reactions will be exacerbated by the fact that they've just witnessed the car-bombing/saved someone from drowning/spoken to the Queen, or whatever it is you want them to talk about.

Consideration, tact and sympathy will get you a long way. You may not even notice that you're being patronizing or overbearing, or putting words into their mouths, but they will; and won't give you the authentic response you're after.

If you're in a position to set up an interview beforehand, rather than dashing onto the scene, it may help, whether you're writing or phoning, *not* to use the word *interview*. Interviews are for the famous, as far as the rest of the populace is concerned. They involve being given a hard time by Brian Walden; or flattered by Terry Wogan. The only other connotations the word *interview* has are menacing and unpleasant: interviews with the headmaster; interviews for jobs. Interviews are things you *fail*. Instead, ask them if you may come and talk to them. It's a lot less formidable.

interviewing experts

This is the easy one. Being experts, they just love to talk about it, whether it's gene-splicing or Gene Vincent. An expert will always add lustre and authority to your copy. Credit them carefully. Make sure to check how to spell their names, and get them to give you an exact description of the area of their expertise, their post, professional title, and the organization they represent. Putting 'lecturer' when you mean 'professor', or 'Fan Club' when they prefer 'Appreciation Society', may not make a scrap of difference to your readers or you, but it will to them. Take care, and get it right.

Because you're consulting an expert for facts or explanations, you're clearly under no obligation to know very much yourself. They will love explaining everything to you. On the other hand, it will help the rapport considerably if you show at least a lay understanding of what's involved.

Don't overdo the number of experts in any one feature. Too many, and your reader will start to get cynical. They'll all disagree with each other anyway.

interviewing stars

Since an interview with a star constitutes a feature in its own right, this is probably what you'll be doing most of. The golden rule is:

Never treat the famous as though they are famous. Treat them with respect. Mention, by all means, that you very much admire the book/film/record/spaceflight you're here to talk about; but don't be awed; don't be nervously deferential;

don't be sycophantic. You'll get a much better response if you convince them that you too are a professional, doing a professional job. Follow these guidelines.

Preparation. Get a firm date, time and venue; and make sure you both know how long the interview is going to take. Warn them if your magazine is planning a six-page feature with cover photo; or reassure them that it's only 500 words, so you won't take up much of their time. You should be able to get enough for a 2,500-word piece on one side of a C90.

The date should be well ahead of your deadline, just in case unexpected professional engagements suddenly intervene; or the star has a hangover and simply calls it off.

Research. Know your subject beforehand. Read the books, or a selection advised by someone who *has* read the books; listen to the records and memorize the credits on the sleeve; know what teams they've played for, what goals they scored. Get a biography from their agent, press office, newspaper files or reference books. Don't just read it, learn it. Get as many dates into your head as you can.

All this will pay off in fluency of communication, at least inasmuch as there will certainly be problems if you get their marriages in the wrong order, attribute a rival director's movies to them, or forget about their Olympic gold medal. Fame does funny things to the personality. Stars' egos can be as vulnerable as they are inflated. Convince them they're in safe, knowledgeable hands, and they will hold forth.

Questions. Some professional interviewers, especially those who have to deal with a great number and variety of respondents, make a great point of having a script and sticking to it; and making the respondents stick to it too, even when that means cutting them short or pressing them to answer something. A detailed list of questions definitely ensures you get what you came for, and waste no time. Some interviewees will be reassured to see you've got a list of questions, evidence that you have done some preparation.

Others prefer to chat about whatever comes along. You get a more natural self-presentation this way, though it's not guaranteed you'll get beneath the surface defences, and will only encourage poseurs, or those hiding behind a façade.

Perhaps the best thing is to have a list of half-a-dozen important questions, and run through them until the conversation takes off in its own direction. Return to it as necessary to make sure you cover all of them, in whatever order. It seems a bit dumb to demand that your respondent answers question three when in fact, at that moment, she's bursting to tell you all about question five, which she hasn't even seen yet. After all, it doesn't matter how you get the information out of them, as long as *you* don't dry up. So it helps to have something written down.

Tact and diplomacy. These speak for themselves. You'll find stars respond differently to different interviewers from different publications. If experience has told them that you or your magazine is likely to interrogate them ruthlessly or even caricature them in print, they'll clam up. If they think you're a considerate person and your magazine has nothing to gain by attacking them, they'll be more expansive. If you *do* have awkward or potentially explosive questions to ask, start off with the innocuous ones and wait for your moment.

In general, you'll find that rising stars are more communicative than the very famous, not least because they need the publicity. They'll answer anything, where megastars will be more choosy. If you're dealing with agents, record companies or PR outfits that handle a whole spectrum of stardom, you can often bargain your way to an interview with a Big Name by spending time talking to the lesser fry they're anxious to push.

Location. Whatever PR agents believe, the best place to interview a recording artist is *not* in a studio, or a film actor on a set. Of course it will add local colour to your piece; but it will also waste your time and bore you rigid while you're waiting for them to have time to talk to you; and when they do, they'll be distracted by the demands of their work. There is nobody more tense and belligerent than an actor between takes, especially if they're takes 54 and 55 respectively.

The place to interview celebrities is in hotels, in tearooms, in neutral offices, in *quiet* restaurants and wine bars: well away from the stress and frustration of the actual workplace.

However: I once interviewed Dire Straits' frontman Mark Knopfler in the Warwick Hotel in Paris. The tape was rolling, we were relaxed and getting on with it, when suddenly a resident pianist materialized and struck up with 'Raindrops Keep Falling on My Head'. Conscious of the fact that the hotel was crawling with music biz personnel, the guy sang his way through a vast medley of MOR favourites in an attempt to impress. We fell about laughing. The interview went fine, but transcribing the tape was torture.

'I like interviewing people in hotel lobbies, because they can't scream and shout and throw tantrums.'

KIM NEWMAN, City Limits

If you do take a star to lunch, you may get an insight into their characters from their table manners and culinary preferences; but do watch what *you* order. It's hard to converse with maximum alertness while you're teasing prawns out of their shells. Choose a dish you can fork casually into your mouth, keeping one hand free for adroitly re-positioning the tape recorder as the waiter stands things on top of it. When I interviewed 'voice-over queen' and actress Miriam Margolyes in a tiny Jewish fish restaurant, she attacked her haddock with her fingers and sucked at the bones while talking loudly about sex and laughing hugely, oblivious to the horror of little old ladies at tables all around. We didn't get thrown out, but the interview was largely unprintable.

writing up interviews

The disadvantage of using a tape is transcribing it later. Writers are unanimous in loathing the task. A personal stereo with headphones and a pause button is probably the most painless machine to use, though there is something to be said for old-fashioned pedal-operated dictaphones.

To transcribe a tape exhaustively will take you, depending on your typing speed about four times as long as the tape itself. It is advisable to transcribe very fully, as you can never be sure exactly what snippets you're going to use, and skipping something doubtful early on in the tape is a sure way of running into something later that you can make sense of only by quoting the earlier bit too. You can leave out a lot of your own side of the conversation, of course.

There are as many ways to write up an interview as there are people to interview in the first place. If you're lucky enough to get someone supremely articulate, you can simply write an introductory paragraph, open inverted commas, and let it roll as a monologue. Even this will require tailoring, as the gap between the spoken and the written word is a dangerous one to skip. However much you find yourself rewriting, you must retain plenty of your subject's habits of speech, loose and ungrammatical as they may look on the page, or you'll come to the end and realize their character has, somehow, mysteriously evaporated en route.

The next step up is the question-and-answer form, pioneered by Andy Warhol's *Interview* magazine, popularized by *Playboy* and *Ritz*, and now taken up by teen magazines and the music press. You quote your own questions (which you inevitably rewrite, prompting many interviewees to wish they had the same opportunity to do the same to their answers). These are printed in a different typeface, bold or italic, and alternated with the replies. The form appears entirely simple and straightforward, though in fact there's room for a good deal of cunning, reorganizing the order of the questions to make it more logical, cutting different parts of the transcript together to sharpen a point, revelation or mannerism, and generally making the thing run much more smoothly than even the most eloquent conversation ever could. Open with a paragraph of introduction, into which you can stitch any interesting odds and ends you've thrown out of the body of the piece. This is Gary Crowley talking to Rupert Everett in *Just 17* (26 June 1985).

❝ *At the moment you reside in both London and Los Angeles. What do you like and dislike about each of those cities?*
I love my house in Chelsea, English people, and I suppose the generally relaxed way of life. I hate British Telecom, British Rail and policemen. As far as LA's concerned, I'm made for Sunset Boulevard, going to the beach and all the great cinemas, but I

don't like the fact that you can't walk anywhere.
Having said that I'm one of the lucky ones and have
a Thunderbird!

The stage success of Another Country *helped to launch you.
Any chance of a return to theatre?*
Oh yes. What I would like to do, and I know not
many theatre people will be into this, is to do a play
and really put the prices up so one or two nights a
week could be free for the unemployed or low-
waged.That's important—subsidised theatre. I want
to get a completely different crowd. Young people
who don't usually go to the theatre. 99

The opposite of the Q-and-A interview is the narrative
form, where the writer relies heavily on his or her own
observations and abilities to bring the respondent to life as a
figure in a landscape, rather than a disembodied monologue
or dialogue. This is a good way of dealing with interviewees
who aren't terribly forthcoming, or don't express themselves
in a very interesting way; but it will involve your taking
careful note of all the relevant things that aren't on the tape:
the interviewee's environment, clothes, behaviour, etc.

Whatever form you choose for your interview, there's
room at the top for a 'hood', as in any other feature. Open
with some intriguing fact you've unearthed. For his profile of
Faye Dunaway in *TV Times* (4 October 1984) Malcolm
Macalister Hall led off with an exemplary piece of research.

66 You might think of Faye Dunaway as sexy,
dangerous, alluring. But in the small town of Pau in
the French Pyrénées, they remember her for
something quite different. The town's main industry is
making berets—an item of headgear which, by the
mid-Sixties, was sadly out of fashion, favoured
mainly by gnarled peasants on old bicycles.

In 1968, though, sales went through the roof—from
1,500 a week to 20,000 a week. All it took was for
Faye to wear a beret in *Bonnie and Clyde* (1967), and
every girl wanted one. If they couldn't have a
machine gun as a fashion accessory, they could at
least get a maxi-skirt and the right hat.

This Sunday, Faye stars on ITV in the first part of
the film *Voyage of the Damned* (1976), a powerful
story about a group of Jews fleeing pre-war Nazi
Germany on a luxury cruiser bound for Cuba.

Today, she lives most of the time in London: she's
still alluring, even in plain navy blue skirt and
jumper. At 43, she's got the odd wrinkle, a charming
smile, and a rented house in the smartest part of
town. 99

The difference between the professional writer and the

neophyte is in the way Malcolm has worked that item about berets in his article, first extending it to a description of what else Dunaway wore in *Bonnie and Clyde*, and then turning directly to what, by contrast, she was wearing on the day.

The Review Columns

If you spend a lot of time reading books, going to movies, galleries, concerts or performances of some kind, and you're knowledgeable and articulate about what you find there, you may be considering making your way into the press via the review columns. It seems like easy money, for saying what you think about something you'd be doing anyway. But there are drawbacks. Your job is to be informative, not opinionated, yet as the *Women's Review* editorial collective point out, 'Reviews which are simply descriptions are not enough.' You have to adapt your style, and even to some degree your judgement, to the publication and what its readers want to read about. You must be concise and pithy, and entertaining even when writing about something that bored you rigid. Yes, you get free tickets or books, but they won't necessarily be things you actually want to see or read. What's more, the background research can outweigh the time and effort of taking in the ostensible subject of your review.

GILLIAN WILCE, *literary editor of the New Statesman:*

66 Book reviewing isn't very cost-effective for a freelance writer. If you add in the time it takes to read the books to the time it takes to write about them, and average it out, it's not a lot per hour. You have to say to yourself that you're going to be reading anyway, so the reading time doesn't count! The fact that the NUJ recommend lower rates for reviewing is probably based on the assumption that people who review books are not freelances, but academics or people with another string to their bow. I haven't found that to be necessarily so. 99

To be a film reviewer, you have to live within easy reach of Wardour Street; to review touring bands or shows, you have to get to their first venue, or give your editor a very good reason why she or he should pay to send you there. Making notes in a darkened theatre is no problem for reviewers of films or plays, who can use a pen-torch or sit in the front row and catch the light from screen or stage; but how are you going to make notes at a rock or pop concert, in a venue with no special provisions for the press and where the only spot with a complete view of the stage is occupied by hundreds of heaving, jostling fans?

If you want to get into reviewing (and very many aspiring writers do), the best way is to study the reviews in your target publication and write one, in an appropriate style, in *exactly* the right form and to the right length, of some current book, film or whatever, and submit it—as a sample, not a submission—to the reviews editor, with a covering letter explaining clearly and briefly who you are, what your relevant background is, what specific areas you're offering to cover and where your writing has appeared.

If you can, propose some forthcoming event or publication that they will want to tell their readers about.

Short Stories

It's not the best of times for the writer of short fiction. It seems that people like to read stories, and people certainly like to write them, but publishers are almost unanimously convinced that anthologies and collections 'don't sell'. It's virtually impossible to place a book of short stories until you've had a reasonably successful novel out, and preferably more than one. For this reason, probably, it's also conventional wisdom that literary agents 'won't touch' short stories; though in fact there are some, like the Deborah Rogers Agency (49 Blenheim Crescent, London W11 2EF (01) 221 3717), who specialize in fiction and actively try to place short stories by writers known and unknown, though the short-term returns are slight indeed. For there's a corresponding shrinkage in the number of magazines publishing any fiction at all; and in the literary magazines at least, a 'name' writer will almost always be preferred to an unknown newcomer.

The healthiest and most stable market for short fiction, provided you're willing to tailor it to the overall requirements of genre and outlet, just as you would writing non-fiction, is in women's magazines.

women's magazines

Like men's magazines, the most upmarket women's glossies, such as *Company* and *Woman's Journal*, tend to publish stylish quality fiction, not necessarily romantic, and usually by famous authors. Aim first lower down the market, where the sphere of literary possibility may be narrower but each magazine has its own idiosyncrasies of outlook, as Barbie Boxall, fiction editor of *Woman's World*, explains.

'At *Woman's World* stories don't have to have a happy ending, but there must be some sort of hope, together with a bit of homespun philosophy—she loses the chap, but the phone rings; or she thinks, "Never mind, everything happens for the best". Something that gives an uplift at the end. They have to have quite a deep emotional content and a strong storyline, so there are often sub-plots.

'I get about sixty unsolicited manuscripts a month. Many of them are much too short. We need about 4–5,000 words, except in the summer when we usually have two stories of about 2,500 words each.

'I did do the fiction for *Look Now* too: obviously that's for much younger readers; and *19*, for instance, has very distinctive fiction. It's rather oddball and a bit offbeat, which doesn't fit the traditional woman's magazine stuff. *19* and *Over 21*'s type of fiction is much more contemporary.

'Weeklies for older women have a much wider canvas. In *Woman* and *Woman's Own* you'll often find stories about old ladies and children, even animals.'

Pat Roberts is fiction editor of *Over 21*. She says: 'Fiction is an important part of the magazine. We look for stories about 3,500 words in length. There are no hard and fast rules. People should read the fiction in the magazine first. 25 unsolicited manuscripts a week take time to read, but we do read them all.'

men's magazines

Because men's magazines cater primarily to male erotic fantasies, many of their readers assume that it will be easy to write down their own fantasies and get them published. In fact, the one thing men's magazines don't need is more pornography. Rupert Metcalf, editor of *Knave*, receives about twenty unsolicited stories a month, of which he buys (for £200) only one in fifty, if that. 'Most of what's offered us as fiction would be more at home in our letters pages,' he says. 'The quality is rarely on a par with what we get from our regular contributors. We're much more likely to accept a well crafted story with no erotic content at all.'

Writing pornography for downmarket magazines can be hard work and much less well paid, as Anne Billson discovered. 'People do seem to think that pornography pays good money, but it doesn't. I've worked for a couple of mags that paid £15 per thousand. Writing porn is very exhausting, and you run out of scenarios very fast.' Upmarket, where it is possible to make a career out of it, the work is still highly demanding, as Debbie Raymond explains.

'I write the fantasy fiction for *Men Only*, and some of the stories for the American version. *Men Only* is the second top-selling magazine in this country, and sells two million a month worldwide. Unlike other magazines, like *Club*, it has an awful lot of fiction and other writing. I call it erotic or filthy fiction. That's exactly what it is, and it's there for one purpose only: to turn somebody on.

'I started with erotic writing and that's all I can write. Everyone thinks they could do it, but it is a skill. And I had to teach myself. It is hard, because you have to make it sexy while keeping a strong storyline going. Most people sit down and string out a list of filthy words, but that won't do. You have to keep the reader occupied, so you can't use the same words over and over again. There are very few storylines, so you have to put things in a different order. Once you get down to sex, there are only a few things you can do, and when it comes to writing about it, there are even fewer things you can do without getting prosecuted. You can only go softer or harder.

'I have to write 2,000 words for the "One Woman's Fantasy" section. It can get really bad sometimes when you've written 1,500 and it's perfect, and then you've got to write an extra 500. You think, what can she do next?'

literary magazines

If you're writing stories for the love of it, rather than aiming at a particular magazine, your chances of publication are much slimmer. There are magazines like the *New Statesman* or the *Listener*, that publish a story once in a while; there's the *London Review of Books*, which publishes about half-a-dozen a year, ideally 3–4,000 words, but longer or shorter on merit—they will serialize. However long your story, they pay a flat rate of £150. The literary quarterly *Stand* might publish up to twenty a year, mostly under 3,000 words, though they don't prescribe a word-limit except for their bi-annual fiction competition, for which entries must be 8,000 or under. Stories must be 'well written but not too glib'.

Women's Review is a different sort of women's monthly, concentrating on women and the arts. They publish one story an issue, usually not longer than 3,500 words, and pay £45 a thousand; but they're overwhelmed with submissions. 'We want stories dealing with women's experience, although anything you might think of sending to *Woman's Own* is probably not suitable for us. As it is, you may have to wait three months before we can get back to you. And do avoid drawing too heavily on other writers. We get far too many copies of Angela Carter.' The *Fiction Magazine* bluntly says: 'We're drowning in paper here. We don't want any more.'

Panurge is a bi-annual paperback with a circulation of about a thousand, dedicated to all kinds of fiction, especially by new writers, and anyone whose writing is not obvious or easy. Stories can be any length, and no standards of professional presentation are required: 'Some of the best stories are atrociously typed on bog paper,' observes editor John Murray, 'a former struggling novelist and short story writer'. *Panurge* is also looking for good literary articles and reviews ('we don't get many, and most of them are abysmal'), and anything good by women. John promises a personal response to submissions 'within days'; and if your story does get printed, it will be read by exclusive agents like Gillon Aitken and publishers like Hamish Hamilton: 'like us,' says John, 'they're fed up with the fact that new writers can't get into the literary magazines, so they watch us keenly.'

Women's Review
Unit 1
1–4 Christina Street
London EC2

Panurge
70 Birks Road
Cleator Moor
Cumbria CA25 5HU

London Review of Books
Tavistock House
Tavistock Square
London WC1H 9JZ

Stand
179 Wingrove Road
Newcastle-upon-Tyne

WRITING BOOKS

Who wants yesterday's papers? Nobody in the world, as the Rolling Stones once observed. Journalism is ephemeral. You can put everything you've got into that hard-hitting, investigative piece on tomato ketchup for *Caterer and Hotel-keeper*, but next month where is it? In the magazine graveyard of the dentist's waiting room. Whereas books are forever. If you'd spent half a year investigating tomato ketchup, and written *The Tomato Ketchup Book* for Octopus, not only might they be shifting thousands in Marks & Spencer, but you could expect to be reviewed in the *Mail on Sunday* and interviewed in *Woman's Own*. Suddenly, and for the rest of your life, you would be the authority on ketchup.

There's something respectable about a book, no matter what it is and where it fits into the literary scheme of things. Even the most craven pulp thriller goes onto the bookshelf after being read, not into the dustbin. To have a book in print may make you a lot of money, or almost none; but what it will always do is turn you magically into a published author, with a status and network of opportunities. Books breed books—maybe not the books you thought you'd write, or even wanted to write, but books none the less.

Just like magazines, there are hundreds of different types of book, and every publisher specializes in a certain well-defined area or areas. It's appalling how many hopefuls with bright ideas or even complete manuscripts waste time and energy pestering the wrong firms. Start with the *Writers' & Artists' Yearbook* by all means; but you'll get further by haunting libraries and bookshops, where books are arranged by subject categories, checking the exact nature of the ones that are most like what you've got in mind, and who published them. There's little point in taking your bright, cheerful, colourfully illustrated *Tomato Ketchup Book* to Christminster University Press, just because they published a *History of Condiments* (3 vols., footnotes) in 1957. It's imperative that you find out exactly what the publisher you're addressing is actually interested in now; and, just as with journalism, that you understand what the process of acquiring books for publication actually entails.

Inside Books

putting a list together

One reason so many amateur authors seem to feel they have a right to be published is that they really don't understand how complicated and time-consuming the business of publishing actually is. Editor after editor will tell you stories of the writer who sent a manuscript in on Monday and rang up on Friday to see if they were going to publish it. The hopeful writer imagines that a publishing house consists of two floors, with an editor upstairs doing nothing but reading manuscripts and occasionally popping one downstairs to the printer. The real picture is very different. As publishing in Britain finally moves away from being a 'gentleman's profession' and individual publishers are subsumed into huge corporate structures, the role of an editor in charge of a list is increasingly executive and managerial. No editor could possibly read his or her own 'slushpile' single-handed. Everyone always estimates that 80–90% of what comes in unsolicited is unsuitable for that firm or, more likely, unsuitable for anyone. The remaining fraction, the possibles, pass through a long process of considerations and decisions:

Profitability

The first thing to realize is that publishers are commercial enterprises. Whatever pieties may be uttered about culture and education when the Chancellor looks like slapping v.a.t. on books, or about upholding our literary heritage when the Booker Prize season wheels around again, publishers exist to make money. Some will treat their authors with extreme civility, some with callous indifference. None will publish your book because they like you, because they see it as an act of charity, or because they think your words are so meaningful that it's only right and proper for the whole world to hear them. They will publish your book only if they feel sure enough people will buy it to make them a profit.

Publishing a book costs thousands of pounds. The actual cost depends on the resources of the company; on what sort of book it is (pulp war novel or definitive encyclopaedia of orchids with five hundred full-colour photographs); on what size of print run it requires; on all the other niceties of production. No one invests thousands of pounds without calculating precisely the percentage they can expect.

Marketability

Is it time to publish your book? Is tomato ketchup a good steady seller? Is it suddenly fashionable? Is it last year's thing? The markets for kinds of novels, too, shift and cycle in peculiar ways. Science fiction is up, westerns are down, romances are holding steady. If the word is that teenage girls are buying books again, editors will be on the lookout for manuscripts suitable for that age-group. This time next year, the very same manuscript might be bounced by publisher after publisher. As fantasy author Gene Wolfe observes, 'The people who do well out of all this are the ones who are just getting on the swings while everybody else is still on the roundabout. Now when the roundabout comes to a stop, you're already there with your manuscript finished, and the others are all scampering for a seat on the swings!'

Market strategy

Every publisher has a well-defined conceptual territory, displayed and advertised by the catalogue of books they hope to publish in any one year. A publisher may have one list or many. Small publishers tend to specialize, while large ones will have a bit of everything they can be sure they can handle. *Mills & Boon*, as everyone knows, dominate the bottom of the women's fiction market with their template romances, some of them written by men. *Virago* publish only female writers, mostly of upmarket fiction and autobiography, and have cornered the market in reissues of forgotten classics. *The Women's Press*, therefore, trade under the slogan: 'Live authors, live issues'. *The Women's Press* are an independent company, while *Pandora*, who also publish a variety of feminist fiction and non-fiction, are the feminist list of *Routledge & Kegan Paul*.

In a larger firm, it's entirely possible for a manuscript to be rejected because it was addressed to the editor of the wrong list, or the right list but at the wrong time.

Acknowledgement

The first thing a publisher should do is let you know that they have received your manuscript: probably with a postcard assuring you it will receive their prompt attention and earliest reply. Don't get excited, this is merely common courtesy. The best response is to put the whole thing out of your mind and get on with something else.

Reading

Very few publishers actually throw any unsolicited manuscripts back without reading a word of them. Apart from anything else, it would be a foolish risk. Anything might be the second Dick Francis. Having creamed off the ones from authors whose names they know, or agents they trust, editors will then read the beginning, middle and end of all the others to separate the few that seem worth a second look from the great bulk of the negligible.

Manuscripts which pass this test will usually be passed to a professional reader, either employed part- or full-time in house, or else freelance and working at home at an agreed fee per hour or per script. This will be someone who knows the editor and the list, who is well read in that general area, and who has proved in some professional capacity (as reviewer, author, or publisher's employee) that they know what does and does not constitute a publishable book. A reader will return manuscripts to the editor with a report on what each contains, its merits and flaws, and a recommendation: to publish or not.

The editorial meeting

An individual editor may have the power and be in the position to accept whatever he or she likes; more commonly, books under consideration will have to be discussed at an editorial meeting. Here, the book suddenly becomes the editor's 'property': he or she will argue the virtues of the book like a defence counsel in a court of law. The better it sounds to the editorial director, financial director, production manager and so on, the more impressive the editor will appear, and the more chance of getting permission to do the book as that editor believes it should be done.

Subsidiary decisions

An editor may want or be asked to get a second or third opinion from another reader, especially if the list is new, in transition, in danger, or made up of highly specialized books. But the most important factor will be financial.

At this point the editor may come back to you, the author, and with many sweet and flattering words, ask whether you might not consider revising your work slightly. 'Marketing are not at all confident about *The Tomato Ketchup Book* for the British market. Would you be interested in doing some more research and broadening it so that they could sell it in America and Australia too?' If a huge investment and substantial planning are involved, there may be another delay while some specific market research is commissioned, conducted, processed and concluded.

Discreet enquiries

If you haven't heard a word since the acknowledgement, and at least two months have gone by, it's now quite acceptable to write a brief and courteous note asking whether your editor will be making a decision soon; and to follow it, if necessary, after a fortnight with a phone call to the same effect. Be diplomatic. The last thing they need, or want, is another difficult author. On the other hand, if your book is obviously topical, or you need a decision straightaway in order to take advantage of some research opportunity, or to get the book revised in time for it to be published for somebody's centenary, or to catch the Christmas novelty book rush, then be *firm*.

Bluff

It may not be wholly ethical but it's quite normal to inflate whatever slender assets you can bring to bear on a hesitant editor. If you happen to know a rival publisher's secretary, and she happens to have mentioned your book to her boss, who happens to have expressed no great antipathy to giving it a cursory glance some time, you may translate this into: 'Look, I don't want to rush you, but X over at Y has already expressed an interest and is keen that I should offer the book to them—if you don't want it, that is.' If you have a canny agent, this kind of routine is best left to them, but it is quite acceptable, because it's the sort of thing publishers are doing themselves all the time.

Acceptance
Any problems have been ironed out, all conditions met, and they make you an offer. It might seem disappointingly meagre to you, especially if this is your first sale and you've got no strong bargaining position, but it may well be negotiable. It's not so much that publishers are out to rob you blind, but they will buy everything *as cheaply as they can*. Here the production budget gets put on the table again. If the estimates show that the book should earn £3,000 from its first printing, then the publisher is likely to offer you, say, £2,000, to allow for both profit and safety margins. There's nothing to stop you from asking for more. Contracts are always negotiable. For more details, see 'Payment for Authors', p. 39.

The Book Business

The good news from the editorial director of Jonathan Cape is that 'the prospects for a new writer looking for a publisher are probably better now than ever before.' Liz Calder was speaking in 1985, when of twenty-one new titles on Cape's fiction list, as many as nine were first novels, including Isabel Allende's. It was Liz Calder who signed up Salman Rushdie and Anita Brookner as unknowns; both went on to win the £15,000 Booker McConnell Prize for Fiction, an annual award which has done much in the last four or five years to revive public interest in the English novel. In the words of Norman St John-Stevas, chairman of the 1985 judges, the Booker Prize 'is not for being "top of the pops"; it's not for providing a riveting yarn or an easy read (though the winner may provide this too): it is for the achievement of making what in the all-too-fallible opinion of the judges is a major and serious contribution to contemporary English fiction.' He nevertheless admitted that the result is 'half crusade and half a sporting event'. The selection of the shortlist and nomination of the winner is always controversial, even when the judges are accused of being too safe and conservative. 1985's winner, *The Bone People* by Keri Hulme, a previously unknown New Zealander, was described by Paul Theroux as 'unreadable' and by another critic as 'complex and multi-layered'. From a shortlist that included such uncontroversial luminaries as Iris Murdoch and Doris Lessing, it was clearly a provocative choice.

Though the Booker Prize has detractors who accuse it of bringing literature down to the level of a beauty contest, it does generate interest and publicity, stimulates publishers to invest in novels, and increases sales enormously. Liz Calder explains: 'I published three of Anita Brookner's novels before *Hotel du Lac*: the sales, while growing with each book, were between 1,000 and 2,000, which is perfectly respectable.

Since winning the Booker Prize in 1984, *Hotel du Lac* has sold over 90,000 copies in hardback in our territory alone.' A rather well-bred romance, *Hotel du Lac* clearly caught the public attention in a way that a less immediately accessible winner like *The Bone People* never would, though sales of that had risen, five months after it won the prize, to ten times its original British print-run of 2,500. *The Bone People*'s British publisher, Hodder & Stoughton, had also published the 1981 prizewinner, Thomas Keneally's *Schindler's Ark*, a similarly heavyweight novel of which they had originally expected to sell 10,000 copies, and ended up selling six times that figure.

Because publishers are eager to snap up promising young writers of 'quality fiction' to be entered for the Booker and the Whitbread Prizes, this area of the book business is visibly inflating even while the overall market for hardback fiction is contracting. In 1985 52,994 titles were published in Britain (over a thousand more than the previous year). 5,845 of these were fiction titles, 3,210 of them new ones (rather than new editions of works published previously). Obviously, they can't all win the Booker, or even benefit from award fever. There are authors making more than they're worth, and others making hardly any money at all. Felicity Bryan of the Curtis Brown Literary Agency says: 'Advances are incredibly high. This is wonderful if you represent one of those high-earning authors, but it has a ghastly effect across the board. Those authors who aren't getting the big advances are becoming very restless. An author who would have been thrilled with an advance of $100,000 is furious that he didn't get the $1m Sally Beauman got for *Destiny*. As writing is such a precarious occupation, authors want to be on any bandwagon that's going.'

Some authors take a long time to break into the big money, as Arrow Books' editor Dyan Sheldon illustrates. 'Somebody like Anne Tyler has written maybe a dozen novels. There was a time when you couldn't give her away, here or in America. She was probably earning something like $2,000 advances for years. Then *Dinner At The Homesick Restaurant* became a big seller in the States, and so her latest, *The Accidental Tourist*, went for $600,000.

'All of a sudden she's leapt from being a nice novelist who's only reasonably established to a bestselling blockbuster who can ride high.'

Though even novelists themselves are apt to wonder who it is that buys hardback fiction, especially now that school and library budgets have been cut right back, some authors are doing very nicely. '*The World According to Garp* sold only 50,000 hardback copies and had the majority of its sale in paperback,' says American author John Irving. His latest, however, *The Cider House Rules*, is up to 300,000 in hardback 'and is still going strong. Somebody's buying those books.'

Before Writing

kinds of book

Have a clear idea of what it is you want to write. If possible, think of different ways you might approach it. The angle can be just as important in books as in magazines, because books are planned, promoted and marketed in categories. Is it fiction or non-fiction? A reference book or a 'how-to' book (like this one)? A historical novel or a bodice-ripper? A shocking thriller or a stocking-filler?

You could emulate novelist Keri Hulme, who spent twelve years writing *The Bone People*, or broadcaster and columnist Paula Yates, who ran amok with a camera in the boudoirs of the young and famous, and published the result as *Rock Stars in Their Underpants*. Doubtful as it may seem to the seasoned collector of rejection slips, publishers will buy *anything* as long as:

- it fits their list
- it's well presented
- they reckon it will make money.

Expert and expensive market research notwithstanding, there are always firms who've guessed wrong about the last point. But nothing makes as much steady money as a solid 'how-to' book. Gardening, cookery and DIY books comfortably outsell all but the most spectacular novels.

non-fiction books

Jinny Johnson is a freelance editor who has worked with firms like Mitchell Beazley and the packager Marshall Editions, producing colourful, popular books packed with information and illustrations, for adults and children. How does her side of the business work?

66 Big publishing companies have to invest heavily in warehousing, marketing and distribution. In order to make the best use of that servicing network, ideally they have to have more books to sell than their creative staff could ever produce. So they buy in books from packagers, who produce them through all the stages from original idea to finished copies, but aren't big enough to maintain marketing and distributing departments at all.

'If we come up with an idea, or a publisher asks us to do a book on something, I may have to find illustrators and writers. I'm drawn more to people who know the subject than people who can write.

'Before a packager does too much on an idea,

they'll want it in a form they can sell here and in the States, and hopefully in Europe as well. First they'll want a plan of *The Tomato Ketchup Book*: a brief rundown of the proposed content, section by section, so many pages a section—what goes into tomato ketchup?; tomato ketchup in different countries; who eats tomato ketchup?

'The title can be very important in selling an idea. The publisher is going to be trying to sell it along with thousands of other ideas at one of these great big book fairs, like Frankfurt. Commerce is all. When you're trying to flog your idea to us, you're really working like an advertising copywriter rather than a prose writer. You have to think of some catchy little phrase—maybe the title, maybe some sort of subtitle—that will stick in people's minds. What we call "riveting facts" are good: *Did you know that there are 315,000 sorts of tomato ketchup?*

'A non-fiction book can be quite a complex thing to put together, and can involve quite a lot of people, so it's easy for it to get far away from the creator's initial thought. If that doesn't matter to you, fine, but if you do want a final say about what goes in, make that understood from the beginning. If it was your idea in the first place, you're in a better position to bargain for a royalty, but it's normal to give a writer a flat fee. I've just paid somebody, a psychiatrist, £1,000 to write 24 pages, up to a thousand words a page. That included a consultation fee. Some people would command more because they're particularly hot on a subject. To produce a big book with a complicated layout, artwork and photographs as well, particularly colour photographs, you're talking about an enormous amount of money. The words are the cheapest part of all these things. If we can fill the space with words, we're winning. Words cost less to produce, less to print, and the people who make the words get paid less. **,,**

Approaching a Publisher

Offering a publisher a book you've written is simple enough. You type it or have it typed, neatly and correctly, put a couple of elastic bands round it, add a brief and courteous letter describing it in a couple of sentences and saying why you think theirs is the right list for it, *enclose return postage*, and pop it in the postbox.

Offering a publisher a book you're only thinking about writing is a different and more complicated task. You have to convince them of several things:

- that it's for them
- that it'll make them money
- that it can be done
- that nobody else has done it already
- that you can do it.

This last is, of course, quite a hurdle. If you've already had a book published, any kind of book, you're halfway there. You've shown you can write a book, work which requires far more organization, concentration and stamina than anybody realizes before they try. If you haven't a published book to your name, you have to persuade the publisher that you know what you're taking on. Do it methodically.

the proposal

This is simply a preliminary letter saying: Look, here's a good idea. Describe the good idea clearly and succinctly, add a paragraph mentioning some of the ways you would develop it, and ask them if they're interested to let you know as soon as possible. Give the impression that you're ready and keen to get started, and let it be understood, without saying so in so many words, that if they're not interested you can soon find someone else who will be. Enclose your phone number *and* stamped addressed envelope.

You can send the same proposal, slightly varied according to circumstances, to several publishers simultaneously. After a week or so, the responses will begin to arrive: No, thank you; Not today; Not for us. Humane and considerate publishers may even suggest other firms you might try.

When someone does bite, arrange a meeting. It's still only an idea, remember, not a property, a duty or a sacred quest. They'll probably be willing to give you a cup of coffee and talk it over with you.

Be clear. Bring your file. Have everything at your fingertips. Take notes.

Whether they do want to meet you yet or not, discussion won't proceed much further without a synopsis.

the synopsis

This is a short document, say 500–2,000 words, outlining the areas the book will cover, showing the argument or structure of the information contained in it. Your synopsis must show that you are planning the book and can conceive it both as a whole, and as a section-by-section breakdown.

portion and outline

The proposal shows you've got an idea; the synopsis shows how you'll develop it; now what they need to know is, can you write? A synopsis and sample of the text usually to together as a package known as a *portion and outline*. An editor will want to see a couple of thousand words to show: (*a*) that you can *write* a couple of thousand words, and seem able to continue; (*b*) what the tone of the book will be.

This is the package they'll want to take into the editorial meeting where decisions will be made to pursue the project or not. After unsuccessful approaches editors and agents may shake their heads sagely over your presentation and announce that it wasn't 'a selling synopsis'.

Portion and outline is a method you can use for selling fiction too, though you're unlikely to sell your first novel this way. With one novel out, or at least in production, a couple of chapters of the next together with a couple of pages spelling out the rest of the plot will usually be enough for an editor to consider whether to follow up the option. Beware, however, of the cheerily encouraging response which avoids commitment.

If they still have reservations find out what they are. Go as far as you can to meet them. If you can't, then you're probably with the wrong firm—and you want to know that before you write the book, not afterwards.

the offer

Every offer, as has been said elsewhere, is theoretically negotiable, in terms if not in amount. If it's your first book, however, you're not really in a position to bargain, unless the timing or nature of the book is obviously going to win it huge sales. In general, the firm will make one modest bid for all rights, and not be interested in discussing it, pointing out that you are an unknown quantity, they're taking a risk because they like the book, they're doing you a favour....

Novice authors are completely vulnerable to this kind of pressure. Remember that if the publisher didn't reckon on making a reasonable profit on your work, they would have rejected it. Start phoning agents, if you haven't done so already. Agents will always be willing to discuss offers; and, whatever you suspect, won't be likely to take you on just to get 10% for doing no work. An agent who believes he or she can get an offer raised probably can; or can get you the same money for more advantageous terms; or slightly less money while retaining very valuable rights for you to sell elsewhere for more.

After Writing

copy-editing

The next you see (or should do) of your manuscript after delivery will be when it has been *copy-edited*: tidied up, made self-consistent and consistent with the house style of the publisher, and marked up for the typesetter. There are plenty of things you can do to help—or hinder—this part of the job, as freelance copy-editor Dave Swinden explains:

'If you know who the publisher will be when you're producing your manuscript, it's definitely worth getting a style sheet from them before you set to work. It's no skin off your nose to stick to '-ize' instead of '-ise', if that's what they always do. It'll save the copy-editor work, and lead to a cleaner manuscript. The cleaner the manuscript, the fewer mistakes there'll be in the typesetting. Nobody ever seems to do these sensible things, but I don't see why they shouldn't!

'As a general rule, don't pre-empt the production style of the book. Don't pre-empt the typesetter's instructions. Word processors that will actually print in italic or bold don't save any work, because I still have to mark up the manuscript; and they can confuse a typesetter, especially if your emphasis is in bold where it will eventually be printed in italic. A typesetter can work only from consistent symbols and instructions. The invariable rule is: underlining for italic, wiggly underlining for bold. That's the only thing they can trust as always being the case.

'Publishers will always tell you they're pressed for time, because they always are. You can't let that pressure spoil your book. Inserts that are handwritten because the manuscript has been delivered in haste slow down the editing. If your insert is more than a couple of lines, it should be typed on a separate sheet, and keyed in to where it is to go. If you don't do that, somebody else will have to do it for you anyway. If you do handwrite a phrase or so, don't use joined-up writing. Every character must be separate and clear. It's no good making your typesetter have to guess. By hurrying something in before it's ready, you end up losing time, because it has to be *made* ready. It's worth phoning up the editor, explaining honestly how far you've got, and asking what they prefer: punctuality or readiness. Deadlines are arbitrary dates anyway.

'Don't use single-spacing. Check that the headings of the sections of your text are consistent in form. And avoid vague cross-reference. "*See below*" is irritating unless the subject is actually coming up in the next paragraph, because it doesn't tell the reader where to find it. The best thing to put is "see p. 000", and write in the page number yourself when you get to page proof stage. Three zeroes allows for books up to 999 pages. If yours is longer than that, use four!

'I'd recommend any author, absolutely unequivocally, to insist on seeing a copy of the edited manuscript. It's much easier to argue over something at manuscript stage than at proof stage. And if the copy-editor has put commas round all your *therefores*, don't be afraid to take them all out again. Copy-editors vary in imagination and skill; some are very hot on little rules, but have no appreciation of language. My principle is not whether something is technically right, but whether it's clear or confusing; and the other justification for changing the form of something, say from two words to a hyphenated compound, is for consistency. There's no inherent merit in one form or another. Some authors make a fuss about things like that that really don't matter, but they accept editing which makes their work clearer.

'Copy-editors do care. Most of us, whatever our level of talent or experience, are conscientious. We open up the first bound copy with trembling fingers, just as you do. We want it to be right. If we do things you disagree with, it's not to be vindictive, or to interfere, but because we're actually trying to help. In fact, in publishing it's the author and the editors versus the rest of the organization. Production people have got other priorities; so have marketing people. Make sure you get on with your editors, because they want to get on with you.'

proofreading

Authors of books should always be sent proofs: *galleys* of the text before it's split up into pages, or *page proofs*. A contract will often state that it's the author's responsibility to read and correct proofs, which will then be compared with proofs read by professional proofreaders. Sometimes, when workloads are particularly heavy, or over the summer when staff are away, publishers will hire freelance proofreaders, so if you find you have an eye for this kind of fine detail, there may be temporary work (often paid at an hourly rate) here for you.

Despite scrupulous copy-editing, errors of all kinds can creep in, especially now that technology is changing faster than operators can be trained to keep up with it. Novelist Shena Mackay once received copies of her latest book with a chapter added from a completely different book! 'It had a character called Seamus in, and so did mine, so they probably thought it belonged there.'

Proofreading is taxing work, regardless of whether you're one of those writers who hates to see their own creations in print or not. You really need to look at every single word, every single *character*, to spot all the mistakes that might be there. Unfortunately, you tend to see what you expect to see, especially when the words are as familiar to you as these surely are by now. The publisher's proofreader will be depending on you to pick up mistakes only you can spot, where what's printed apparently makes sense, but something has actually been omitted or garbled. You'll be asked to mark printers' errors and your own amendments in different colours. If there are too many of the latter, you may find yourself with a bill for their correction, as stipulated in your contract. This is another reason why your copy should be as clean and accurate as possible from the outset.

MARK IN MARGIN	MEANING	MARK IN TEXT
͡ჿ	delete	cross through /
͡ჿ	delete and close up	above and below
(stet)	leave as printed	underneath - - -
(caps)	change to capitals	underneath ≡
(l.c.)	change to lower case	cross through /
(bold)	change to bold type	underneath ⌁
(ital)	change to italics	underneath ──
(rom)	change to roman type	encircle words or letters ○
(c.u.)	close up	link letters or words ⌣
#	insert space	between words or letters
(eq.#)	make space equal	between words
(less #)	reduce space	between words
(trs.)	transpose	between words or letters. Number to clarify
⊐ ⊏	move to left/right	beside word ⊐ ⊏
(n.p.)	new paragraph	before first word of para [
]	no new paragraph	beside word]
(r.o.)	run on paras	joining paras
(spell out)	spell out in full	encircle ○
⌄	insert comma	after word
᾿/᾿ / ˮ/ˮ	insert single or double quotes	beside word
⊙	insert full stop	after word
H	insert hyphen	between words
(em)	insert dash	between words or phrases
(t.b.)	take back to previous line	enclose word or phrase ⊃
/	end of correction (insert after each mark in margin)	

Novels

MARIO PUZO'S GODFATHERLY RULES FOR WRITING A BESTSELLING NOVEL

I
Never write in the first person.
II
Never show your stuff to anybody. You can get inhibited.
III
Never talk about what you are going to do until after you have done it.
IV
Rewriting is the whole secret to writing.
V
Never sell your book to the movies until after it is published.
VI
Never let a domestic quarrel ruin a day's writing. If you can't start the next day fresh, get rid of your wife.
VII
Moodiness is really concentration. Accept it because concentration is the key to writing.
VIII
A writer's life should be a tranquil life. Read a lot and go to movies.
IX
Read criticism only in the beginning. Then read novels to learn technique.
X
Never trust anybody but yourself. That includes critics, friends and especially publishers.

Writing a book of 50,000 words or more is a mammoth task, and if it's your first then it will rightly be a daunting prospect. Days, weeks, months, even years lie ahead where you will be doing nothing except working on *that bloody book*. It hangs over you like morning fog. It gets in the way of your social life, your leisure activities, your love life. At times you will hate that book and dread the very thought of sitting at the typewriter. Then when it's going well, you'll love and adore it and won't want to stop for anything.

Many authors have to take on journalism or hackwork of some kind in order to finance their novels. Writing on 'The Price of Authorship' in the *Literary Review*, Geoffrey Wheatcroft pinpointed the difficulties precisely:

❝ By the time Macmillan paid me £5,500 I had left the *Spectator* to write the book and support myself as a freelance. I thought I had enough money to write the book, but I hadn't. It didn't occur to me that I could make a living as a freelance; but I could. The trouble was that whenever one tried to get on with the book one ran out of money, and whenever one took on freelance work one fell behind with the book. The author is torn and crushed between publisher and bank manager. ❞

Some novelists can't write at all unless they're miles away from anywhere. Others can't handle the insecurity of a life without a guaranteed income, and simply must have a full-time job as well. When writing *The Thorn Birds* Colleen McCullough worked eight hours a day as a research surgeon at Yale. 'I used to come in at 7 p.m.and then sit down at the typewriter. I'd work all night and continue like that for days, and then finally I'd crash out.'

What the work is, what the novel consists of, is of course entirely up to you. But there are two projects that seduce the inexperienced writer time and time again—the autobiographical novel and the bestseller.

the autobiographical novel

❝ Most first novels are disguised autobiographies. This autobiography is a disguised novel. ❞

CLIVE JAMES, *Unreliable Memoirs*

It is all too easy to assume that just because you've had an interesting life, you can write an interesting novel. All too often the result, egged on by friends and relations, merely resembles the monologue of the bar-room bore. It's with these sagging manuscripts, and a pocket full of rejection slips, that the doomed finally wander into the vampiric clutches of the vanity publisher.

Read some autobiographical novels. Clive James's *Unreliable Memoirs*, Jeanette Winterson's *Oranges Are Not the Only Fruit*, E. L. Doctorow's *World's Fair*, Alexander Kaletski's *Metro*, James Joyce's *A Portrait of the Artist as a Young Man*—all show the high degree of subtle skill required to turn experience directly into fiction, capturing *and* communicating its essence. J. G. Ballard left his own childhood experience in a Shanghai prison camp to mature for forty years before turning it into the vivid and popular *Empire of the Sun*, coming to the autobiographical novel by way of nine other novels and several books of short stories. Are you really ready to write about yourself, the person you know most intimately and least objectively, before you've learned to write about anyone else?

If you're still determined, write out two notices in big letters, then pin them up above your typewriter where you'll see them every time you roll in a new sheet of paper: *INTERESTING TO WHOM?* and *THINGS ARE NEVER THE SAME WRITTEN DOWN.*

the bestseller

66 Novel writing is to do with the magic of the storyteller, which goes back centuries to when people told stories around campfires, in the woods. You need great characters, whether they are good or bad; and the skill is in the telling of the story. Once you tell a story well, people are hooked.

'I have written a series of twelve novels following the fortunes of two families. In the first book I had them marry; in the second I gave them some children. I knew if I could get people to read the first two, I would be home and dry. That's how it worked out. We've sold millions of them. Borrowing alone has approached $1\frac{1}{2}$ million in the last two years.

'All it is, is the huge human hunger for stories.' 99

CLAIRE RAYNER

With respect to Claire Rayner, hunger is not all it is, neither the audience's hunger nor your own. Apart from 'rogue' bestsellers that nobody could have predicted, like J. R. R. Tolkien's *The Lord of the Rings* or Sue Townsend's *The Secret Diary of Adrian Mole Aged $13\frac{3}{4}$*, bestsellers are planned, constructed and marketed with a high degree of calculation and a nicety of commercial judgement. Sales figures, as we all know, don't necessarily reflect quality, but nor do they necessarily reflect potential popularity either. More and more they reflect efficiency and cunning.

Still keen? Then read Bryan Appleyard's article 'How to Write a Winner' in *The Times* (8 February 1986).

66 First of all the book has to be long. Anything less than 150,000 words is a waste of time as is anything less than 10 major characters.... Along with length goes scope. Publishers feel more secure if they can describe a novel as 'panoramic' and/or 'sweeping'—it suggests value-for-money ... Love affairs are conducted 'against a backdrop' of, for example, the Second World War. For complete escapism it may be necessary to go for something a little more nebulous like 'the glamorous cut-throat world of fashion and the fashionable' as a backdrop. But either way one needs the gratifying impression that a whole world is crammed between the covers. 99

This compendiousness entails elaborate plotting and lots of detail; lots of romantic sex too, designed with the predominantly female audience in mind, and a smooth, rhythmical but undemanding style to keep them turning all those 400-plus pages.

Getting Started

Whatever you're writing, getting off the ground takes the most energy. Some authors plunge in wherever their imagination beckons, and trust the magic. Even this can be nerve-wracking. 'I hate starting,' admits Colleen McCullough. 'I think it's something to do with the artist's fear that this time the magic may not be there; that you've lost it.'

Arthur Hailey couldn't be more different. He says: 'I always take three years over a book. Having decided on a general subject area, I do nothing but travel and research and find out about the background for the first year. I then have an enormous number of notes and I spend the next six months planning what I am going to write. I write an outline of the main characters, the theme, and then the sub-plots and the secondary characters. I wind up with an outline of 50–60 pages of single-spaced writing: writing which never sees the light of day, but which nevertheless is my road map for the long journey of writing which lies ahead.'

Perhaps it was Arthur Hailey that John Fowles had in mind when he wrote, scornfully: 'It is only innately mechanical, salami-factory novelists who set such great store by research; in nine cases out of ten, what natural knowledge and imagination cannot supply is in any case precisely what needs to be left out.'

First Sentence

Opening sentences are extremely important. After the publisher's blurb, the opening sentence is the first thing a prospective buyer reads.

Scattered through the rest of this section you'll find the openings of a number of different novels. Notice the ones that grab your attention, and why. Notice too how many of them announce clearly the sort of novel they are.

66 It was love at first sight. The first time Yossarian saw the Chaplain he fell in love with him. 99
JOSEPH HELLER, *Catch-22*

66 In a hole in the ground there lived a hobbit. 99
J. R. R. TOLKIEN, *The Hobbit*

66 Whenever Henry Wilt took the dog for a walk, or, to be more accurate, when the dog took him, or, to be exact, when Mrs Wilt told them both to go and take themselves out of the house so that she could do her yoga exercises, he always took the same route. 99
TOM SHARPE, *Wilt*

66 'How long have we been sitting here?' I said. I picked up the field glasses and studied the bored young American soldier in his glass-sided box.
  'Nearly a quarter of a century,' said Werner Volkmann. 99
LEN DEIGHTON, *Berlin Game*

66 Once you have given up the ghost, everything follows with dead certainty, even in the midst of chaos. 99
HENRY MILLER, *Tropic of Capricorn*

66 All nights should be so dark, all winters so warm, all headlights so dazzling. 99
MARTIN CRUZ SMITH, *Gorky Park*

66 It was five o'clock in the afternoon when I woke up. The room stank of stale cigarettes and cheap sour red wine. 99
HAROLD ROBBINS, *Dreams Die First*

66 On a cold and overcast Thursday in March of 1850 my mother was laid to rest in Highgate Cemetery, and on that same day I met my cousin Niles. 99
LEONIE HARGRAVE, *Clara Reeve*

66 It was a bright cold day in April and the clocks were striking thirteen. 99
GEORGE ORWELL, *Nineteen Eighty-Four*

66 Like most people I lived for a long time with my mother and father. My father liked to watch the wrestling, my mother liked to wrestle; it didn't matter what. She was in the white corner and that was that. 99
JEANETTE WINTERSON, *Oranges Are Not the Only Fruit*

66 Cadillac sat on the ground near Mr Snow and listened with half-closed eyes as the white-haired, bearded old man told the naked clan-children the story of the War of a Thousand Suns. 99
PATRICK TILLEY, *Cloud Warrior*

66 The sky above the port was the colour of television, tuned to a dead channel. 99
WILLIAM GIBSON, *Neuromancer*

66 They're out there. Black boys in white suits up before me to commit sex acts in the hall and get it mopped up before I can catch them. 99
KEN KESEY, *One Flew Over the Cuckoo's Nest*

In 1983, in California (where else?), a competition was held to find the worst opening sentence for a novel. It attracted ten thousand entries from over fifty countries. The winner was Gail Scott, by day a technical writer for the Bank of America, who had written:

66 The camel died suddenly on the second day, and Selina fretted sulkily and, buffing her already impeccable nails—not for the first time since the journey began—pondered snidely if this would dissolve into a vignette of minor inconveniences like all the other holidays spent with Basil. 99

The ironic thing about this jawbreaker is that 'The camel died suddenly on the second day', *full stop*, would have made a wonderful beginning. The urge to rush breathlessly on completely ruins the effect.

SF writer John Brunner advises beginners always to start with motion. Motion carries your reader (and you) straight into the action. However you begin, with a modest murmur or a piercing shriek, with a silly walk or a left hook, you have to establish your tone directly, excite your reader's curiosity, and persuade them: *now read on*. Opening sentences are an aperitif to the hunger for stories.

Output—How Much?

Authors are capable of feats of phenomenal rapidity, but also of painstaking gradualism. The more of them you ask, the more different answers you get. Jackie Collins produces ten pages of longhand, about 3,000 words, a day. Len Deighton says he is a 'very slow writer, as I throw away a lot of material,' but still manages 2,000 words on a good day and 'nothing on a bad day.' Frederick Forsyth produces 4,000 words between 9.30 am and 1.30 pm, then goes over it after lunch and a stroll. Jack Higgins once managed 12,000 words in 24 hours, but averages around 3,500. When pushed for time and money Michael Moorcock once notoriously wrote a trilogy in nine days ('45,000 words a book, 15,000 words a day'), and claims never to have read the result! Celia Brayfield, author of *Glitter*, says: 'I can feel comfortable doing 5,000. I once did 10,000 when I was late finishing a book. I think the hardest part of writing is organizing the ideas. Once I know what I want to say, I don't have the slightest problem saying it.'

Arthur Hailey, on the other hand, says: 'I'm a very slow writer. I used to write a paragraph at a time, with a ballpoint pen, then put it into a typewriter and go over it again and again. I might change it ten times before I am satisfied and will move on to the next paragraph. My output is still around 600 words a day.' While Colleen McCullough, intriguingly enough, observes: 'Once I sit down at the typewriter you won't get me off the chair, except to have a coffee or a tinkle, for at least ten hours. If it's straight narrative, I can write 10,000 words in a session. If it's a love scene, it'll take me four weeks to write 300 words!'

Rules

The evidence we've accumulated so far, confirmed by books like John Haffenden's *Novelists in Interview*, Alan Burns and Charles Sugnet's *The Imagination on Trial* and Charles Platt's *Dream Makers*, is that every novelist is a law unto herself or himself, sharing nothing but knowledge of the loneliness of the long-distance writer.

generic rules

Genres of fiction are like kinds of sport. Fans of football expect and enjoy different things from fans of golf; and lawn tennis is distinct from court tennis, real tennis or table tennis. So, if you're writing a romance, or a horror story, there are certain things you can't do without disappointing, confusing or annoying your readers, and certain things you *must* do, to sustain their attention and give them the kind of pleasure they were anticipating when they gravitated to that special section of the bookshop, and to your book in particular.

Romantic fiction must be about the awakening and growth of love between people. There are sub-genres of lesbian and gay romance, but the great majority of the romance-reading public will expect the story of a hetero-sexual affair, addressed to a female reader even if told from the male viewpoint. It can be happy, painful, straightfor-ward or complicated; but it must describe the development of that love through recognizable stages in a credible sequence. If you fumble that, you're out of the game.

Horror novels must be about the violation of the everyday by uncontainable and emotionally unacceptable figures and forces. That's your basic game, whether it's the tale of Granny's ghost or of loathesome, pulsating worms that creep up through the wastepipe of the loo. Horrors may arrive as retribution for wickedness, or merely signal that the cosmos is all vile and disgusting anyway. But if your horrors are too feeble, or your picture of normality too flimsy and negligent, the frisson won't spark, and your reader will swiftly go back to Stephen King.

Political thrillers, sword and sorcery epics, titillating chronicles of affluence and sleaze, all have implicit rules, about how their characters and landscapes are to be depicted and what it is about them that is of interest: their intellects? their stamina? their hair-dos? If you're writing genre fiction, take the trouble to find out what the rules are, and you'll start to score.

general rules

Nothing discourages a reader more than monotony. Description of people unrelieved by dialogue, or by description of scenery, soon becomes boring. Description of scenery in obsessive, minute detail, unrelieved by any action, soon becomes boring. Description of action, unrelieved by any pause for breath or thought, soon becomes exhausting. Similar sorts of action following one another inconsequentially grow dull and unconvincing. Characters in amateur novels seem always to be making cups of coffee and tea and lighting cigarettes. Dialogue where the speakers can't be told apart confuses and dissuades a reader. Fiction must have rhythm, to keep us going, and variety, to keep us from going to sleep.

sex—the rules of the game

Sex, as Colleen McCullough testifies, can be extraordinarily difficult to write. 'It's just that sex is a non-verbal activity. And how many times has it been described in a book? I just try to find that magic phrase that nobody else has used before, and invariably end up writing about 150 drafts.' The lesson here is that there *are* rules, not rules of license and censorship, but rules of what's appropriate to what you're writing. The novels of neo-beatniks like Kathy Acker and jet-setters like Jackie Collins couldn't be further apart, yet both employ generous quantities of steamy and colloquial sexual language. Does that suit your novel, or would restraint, suggestion, reticence be more in keeping, and even more expressive than intimate glandular detail? How do you write about sexual activities you've never experienced, perhaps never *can* experience? If you've never swallowed sperm, how can you describe its taste convincingly for those of your readers who have?

humour—writing for a laugh

Comic writing defies codification. People who do it well are least good at telling how it's done; witness Alan Coren:

“ I've never really thought about it, I just do it. You can't go about it mechanistically, it's either funny or it isn't. You'll never find out how people do it because they don't know how they do it, and there aren't that many people doing it anyway. It is impossible to analyse what makes writing funny. You just take the typewriter cover off and you pray. **"**

So be pragmatic. Show what you've written to a good selection of people. See how many of them laugh.

children's fiction

Because a child's grasp of the English language is limited, it is logical to assume that since a writer's grasp of the English language is infinitely greater, then writing for children is easy-peasy lemon-squeezy. It isn't.

The snag is children don't read particularly well and their concentration span is next to zero. Also, parents buy the books not the children, so instead of what the child wants to read it's very often what the parents think the child ought to be reading. And parents are obsessed with the idea that the book is doing the child some good.

You cannot write down to a child. And you cannot write up. Because a child will hate you either way. If you patronize him then he will think 'I know that', if you write over his head then he has the embarrassing task of saying 'Mummy, I can't understand that'. It is imperative that you isolate the age group you are writing for precisely.

The younger sector of children's publishing is dominated by the lavishly-illustrated learning or fairy-tale book, where we have a big problem. I can write: 'Princess Ophelia lives in a big castle on a hill' in three seconds. It will take the illustrator a day to illustrate that. Who gets the most money?

It isn't exactly what you would call writing either. Look at the *Mr Men* books. Is there anybody who can't draw a circle and put two legs, two arms and a smile on its face? I doubt it. But the *Mr Men* books have been incredibly successful— forget about the copies sold, what about the merchandising?

As children get older they get into 'adventures' and more exciting writing along the lines of Enid Blyton's *Famous Five* or *Secret Seven* series, or *Just William*. Children love this and like to read about people their own age doing wild things.

Sue Townsend's *The Secret Diary Of Adrian Mole Aged 13¾* was cleverer than Enid Blyton in that she scored on two levels, although I don't think she realized this when she was writing. What she did was exactly the same as what the children's programme *Tiswas* did on TV. She appealed to both children, who adored it, and adults, who were amused by it. And taught us all a lesson in how to market a book.

When writing a book for children: ● Do explain things but don't patronise them ● Use their language ● Be educational ● Don't feel guilty about starting with 'Once upon a time ...' It works ● Make sure good always triumphs over evil.

Rewriting

66 Putting down on paper what you feel is but the beginning, the creative part and the easy part. The difficult bit comes when you have to work at what you have written, hone it, polish it until you have a real work of art. When I put this point to one writer of two novels she turned to me and said: "I'm an artist not a bloody craftsman." "Too bad," I replied, "you'll never make a good artist." Number three was never published, and she never has. 99

PETER DAY, *publisher's reader*

Bestsellers Talking

Tom Sharpe is Britain's most popular funny writer. His novels are zany tales full of the most eccentric characters, with potent social comment underlying their ludicrous plots. His first, *Riotous Assembly*, spoofed the South African police state; *Wilt* told the catastrophic story of a disillusioned polytechnic teacher; and *The Throwback* chronicled a young man's quest to get even with his father and the world at large. Sharpe's twelve novels have sold four million copies between them.

In his mid-fifties, Tom Sharpe looks younger; and more like a minister (which his father was) than a bestseller.

66 I don't look like the person who writes my books. I wanted to be one of those deadly serious writers, like Thomas Mann, or Graham Greene. But it didn't work out. You always get what you deserve. I guess I'm a comedian. You learn what you are and to stay with what you are.

'The original strategy that I had was to write six books. I didn't think I'd make any money for six books, until I'd got the back list going. In fact *Wilt* was my sixth book. Not only are you introducing new books but you have to have the back-up. If people like one of your books they immediately start to look around for another one.

'I write farce. I write rubbish, but I mean that with a sense of irony and an awful lot of hard work goes into that rubbish. To be a bit serious, they are attacking apartheid and I hate apartheid and racism, and sexism. I hope that loathing comes across in my books.

'Half the things in my books are true to life. I maintain that I am writing a form of realism in that real life is as dotty as my books are. I was writing for

years before I developed this style. And then I wasn't
a journalist, I was a photographer. I took babies and
weddings and things.

'I'd been out of South Africa for nine years when I wrote
Riotous Assembly. I was deported because of a play I
wrote about the place, and then I worked in a Technical
College teaching for nine years. The book started out as a
short story and I just kept on writing. I wrote 110,000
words in three weeks and that's bashing the stuff out.

'I remember getting to bits and thinking, what the hell
happens next?, but out it came. I wrote *Wilt* in a fortnight
but most of the other ones—*Porterhouse Blue, Indecent
Exposure*, and *Blott On The Landscape*—were hewn out of
solid rock. I don't think there is a writer like me anywhere
and that's without conceit, you understand.

'I like to work in the garden shed. It's got a heater and
a plasterboard lining, and I feel the need to go out to
work in a morning. I usually only write in the mornings. I
have 14 typewriters and two word processors (in the
study) and write as much as I can depending on my mood.

'My wife reads my manuscripts page by page to give me
moral support. If I get stuck we talk it over and if she says
it stinks I throw it out the window. If my missus doesn't
like it, it's got to be lousy.

'The funny thing about reviewers is that they never
know what the hell to say. They are always comparing me
with people who are completely wrong. A comparison
with Wodehouse is ludicrous. They either hate me or they
love me and I think that's the public reaction too. But if
any writer tells you they never read the critics, then you
can bet the bastard is lying. Some of my reviews have been
harsh; my god, I've had sledgehammer ones. When I say
people don't like me, I mean it.

'When I wrote *Ancestral Vices*, Peter Ackroyd of the
Sunday Times got right under my skin. He went for me in
a nasty, vicious way. It's the only time I have ever replied
to a critic. He accused me of being a pornographer.

'I don't ask people to like my books, just to read them
and judge them on their own merit. One guy gave *The
Throwback* about five columns of well-reasoned argument
about how he hated it. He ended by saying, 'There may be
a worse book published this year, but I doubt it.' I didn't
mind that at all because he'd read the book and argued his
case well. That's fair enough. If you are at all sensitive or
squeamish then you shouldn't read the damn things.

'I read all sorts of writers. I like detective stories—I'm
always saying I don't but I do. It's dangerous because if a
writer's got a particular style it can affect my own. That's
why I read neutral stuff. I don't think you need too much
input to write what I write, if you've got that sort of
imagination to start with. When people ask me what I
write, I say I don't know what I write, I just write. 99

Jackie Collins   **❝**I've always written since I was a kid. I dropped out of school at 15 and consider myself a street writer because I taught myself. I always said I wanted to be a writer but my parents discouraged me. They said, "Oh no, you can't be a writer without any qualifications. You have to go to college," which is rubbish.

'I never dreamed I would get published, but finally I wrote *The World Is Full Of Married Men*, which seemed to me to be a great title. It was about the double standard—how men were allowed to screw around whereas women had to stay at home cooking and looking after the kids. It was a very provocative theme for 1969. Women weren't writing about sexual equality then, they were still writing about having nervous breakdowns in the Cotswolds.

'*Married Men* attracted a lot of publicity—they said it was the filthiest book they'd ever read—and there were no four letter words in it!—and it shot to the top of the *Sunday Times* bestseller list.

'And I haven't looked back, thank God. I love writing, but I don't write to write a bestseller. I don't put sex on page four, put sex on page twenty, and that's a bestseller. I write because I genuinely love it and I write what I want to write. I write about very strong women. They are strong like men. I write about those women who go out and do things, who have great careers, great sex lives and live their lives like men do.

'People don't want to read about the girl next door. They want to read about a character who they dream of being. When they are stuck selling cosmetics on the counter at Woolworths they think—Wouldn't it be great to be like her! I'd love to have furs and jewels and be driven around in a Roller.

'I think when you write books you must be prepared to step back when they are going to be made for TV or movies. It's too difficult unless you are in total control. If I was going to script it, I'd want to direct it and be totally involved, which is impossible in Hollywood unless you're Barbra Streisand.

'*Hollywood Wives* has caused such a shock over here that for two years being a Hollywood Wife has been two dirty words. *Lucky* was released last year and focuses on Hollywood husbands. It's selling well. I was working until about 3 every morning to get it finished. I do work a heavy schedule though. I start at 9 a.m. and will usually work until 5 p.m. When I'm close to deadline I will work late, and weekends too. Once I'm under way I can write solidly for hours. I go to my huge, light, Beverly Hills study and lock myself in. I might move outside to the poolside if I feel like it. And I'm always stalking about the house drinking endless cups of tea. I also have music blaring in the background. I love to listen to soul music while I'm writing: people like Teddy Pendergrass, Wilson Pickett and Al Green. I use music to create a mood.

'I can't start writing unless everything on my desk is in its proper place. I write in longhand in a W.H. Smith foolscap exercise book. I hate word processors because I always like to have physical proof of what I've written. And I always keep a copy of the manuscript in a steel box, in case of fire.

'Personally, I don't care about reviewers and critics. All I care about is that there are people out there reading and enjoying my books. If I get a lousy review, then I put it down to the reviewer being a failed novelist. I've written nine books in eighteen years. That's hardly an overnight success. It's been hard work. And it's only over the last few years that I've really taken off in America.

'*Chances* was the third bestselling book in America in 1982 and *Hollywood Wives* has been phenomenal, selling over 7 million in the US alone. I think the fact that I was here in America getting behind my books was important. You can't just come over here for a few weeks and go home. A book is like a child, you have to look after it and give it a good start in life. I write American books, so I thought I should spend time here. **99**

Arthur Hailey   **66** I have written stories ever since I was a small boy in England. When I left school at fourteen, I wanted a job on the local paper, but they wouldn't give me one: I had no Higher Level Certificate, for the simple reason that my parents hadn't enough money to keep me at school. I joined the RAF in 1939, and later became a pilot, and stayed on until 1947. During that time I wrote short stories which were published, but never enough to make a living out of. But that was always what I wanted to do. In 1947 I emigrated to Canada, and tried again for a job on a newspaper, in Toronto; but they said to get a job I'd need newspaper experience. So I sold real estate for a while. Eventually I did get a job as an assistant editor, and later as editor, on a trade magazine called *Bus and Truck Transport*.

'Then I wrote a play for TV, and suddenly my life turned over. I was swamped with offers of work, and I went on writing for TV for a couple of years. Then a friend at Doubleday asked me to novelize one of my plays *Flight into Danger*. I thought, no, I couldn't do it; so they came up with a collaborator, or rather two who worked together under the pseudonym John

Castle. They used my background and dialogue and storyline; and when I saw the book, my first thought was, why didn't I do it myself? Then Doubleday asked me to write another novel from another of my plays. That was the final straw! I became a full-time novelist. On my own. In my own right.

'I write on a computer now. I might change what I've written eight or ten times before I move on to the next piece, so usually by the time it's finished I've got it as good as I can make it. Halfway through my latest, *Strong Medicine*, I went over to an IBM display writer, which is bigger than the personal computer. I use it for everything: to keep track of royalties, bank accounts, investments, my wine list—everything. I am addicted to it.

'I have never had any problems with book contracts, but I've dealt with Doubleday throughout my career, and we've never had the slightest argument over money in 25 years. They are a completely ethical company. I did have an agent in the early years, a wonderful woman. She died in 1973, and since then I have managed my own career, except for TV and films, where I still have an agent. It's a jungle where no writer should walk alone. *Strong Medicine* is the eighth book of mine to be made into a film. I look on it philosophically. At first I did get involved and wrote a couple of screenplays, but I realized that being an author involved in a film takes a year of your life, and a year *off* your life.

'I was very happy with the film versions of *Airport* and *The Moneychangers* particularly, but *Wheels* was made for TV, and I had trouble recognizing my own story. I tell people: the book is mine, judge me by that. If you like it, praise me; if you hate it, blame me.

'I've never coveted power, and writing is all I ever wanted to do. At the same time, I still suffer the agony of facing a blank screen. My wife describes it as a love-hate relationship. I suppose that is pretty accurate. When a piece of writing is done, or when you're halfway through it and it is going well, there's no other feeling like it. **99**

Colleen McCullough **66** *Tim* was my bash at the love story, *Thorn Birds* was my bash at the epic, and *Indecent Obsession* was my bash at the whodunnit—which nobody spotted at all. I think *A Creed for the Third Millennium* is my bash at the political thriller.

'Writing doesn't run in the family. But I was writing novels at the age of five. Of course they were very short, but as I became older, the novels got longer. I must have written hundreds of them in longhand in an exercise book.

'It always irked me that I wrote by longhand, and I wanted to see my work on the printed page like real books. When I was fifteen my mother gave me some money to go into town and buy an overcoat. I came back with a portable typewriter. From that day on I have typed every word that I have written. The thing about longhand is that it intrudes my own personality between what I've written and my analysis of it: my ability, after it's written, to stand by and criticize it and see it as it should be seen.

'That's why I craved to see my work in print. I never tried to publish; I just wanted to see what I'd written without my handwriting intruding. Once I'd got a typewriter—what bliss. The typewriter is a very important step forward. It's also far cheaper than exercise books once you've got the initial outlay out of the way. I'm an obsessive-compulsive. I'm a very neat typist and taught myself. A very clean, accurate typist, with two fingers.

'By profession I'm a trained scientist so I'm not afraid of technology, but I have never used a word processor. A word processor is a tool for somebody whose technique of writing is far different from mine. I'm a very good grammarian so I don't need a machine to correct my grammar or spelling and I don't switch paragraphs or sentences around. For me, an ordinary old typewriter is just as efficient.

'Also, the more complicated a piece of equipment is to use, the more likely it is to go wrong. I live 1,100 miles from the nearest typewriter repair man, so buying a word processor is something I have to think about. But if I have to write and don't have my typewriter, I will even write in longhand.

'After *Thorn Birds*, when I was writing full-time, a lady of leisure, I discovered that even though I had the time, during the day you're the victim of interruptions—the bloody telephone, and staff, and visitors. I don't have the temperament to be rude to people, so rather than that I've stuck to nightwork. I work all night. I love the solitude of working at night, with words.

'I think about my books for a long time before starting. I'd rather do anything than start a book. I'd rather go to the dentist. Apart from the feeling that I might have lost the magic, there's the realization that once I've started, then I'm in for a very long slog. But once I do sit down at the typewriter and start, then the dread is all over; the magic is there and I'm away. You can let a bomb off in the same room, but once I'm concentrating, that's it. I don't hear anything, I don't see anything, all I can do is write.

'My dream is to have a certain room. You'd think

after becoming a millionaire I would have this lavish study with all mod. cons., but it never happens like that. Somehow everything I write gets written on a kitchen table. **99**

Peter York **66** I'm very poor guidance to any would-be writer. A lot of things have been luck and happenstance. So don't do as I do!

'I'm a full-time business chap and a hobby writer. I'm a market researcher. If you do that sort of work, you are writing for a living already: interpretation, analysis, defining the agenda; and you write a lot of reports. So I was pushing words around before I started writing proper.

'*Harpers & Queen* gave me the opportunity to write in a consumer magazine. How it happened hardly comes under the category "recommended practice". At a party I met Ann Barr from *Harpers*, so I said, "I can do that, gizza job." She said, "Come up with some ideas and we'll see." The first thing I did for *Harpers* was spend half a day in Barnsley interviewing Arthur Scargill. The next thing, the precursor of it all, was a style piece on New York. Then, with 'Sloane Rangers', the whole thing went bananas.

'Being a market researcher, I rather like typology. 'Sloane Rangers' hit a nerve because of (*1*) the big thing of typology in itself, and (*2*) the story of typology it was. And it became a catchphrase.

'In my writing I felt that I'd hit my stride, and I became more involved in the features side of *Harpers*. I was still a 100% full-time businessman, but writing was a lovely hobby.

'One thing, if you are a certain kind of office chap, is that you have people to type for you. I've never learnt to type, so I either write in longhand or dictate into a machine. In that sense I am not a true writer or reporter. I'd be little use behind the lines in Cambodia. I can't type, I can't do shorthand, and I've never worked on the *Sheffield Telegraph*. I've never done anything proper writers are supposed to do.

'What I am good at, unashamedly, once I've had a good idea, is exerting the maximum possible mileage out of it in terms of presentation and publicity. The fact that *The Sloane Ranger Handbook* is a very successful book and goes far beyond normal books is proof of that. Writers of the old school think that good marketing somehow cheapens the product, but I think that they feel threatened by it.

'I have to say, I read and re-read my work, and think, God, that's good. With *Sloanes*, one has to say *we* were good, because it was a 50/50 enterprise. I am struck dumb with wonder at how well it's done. I think it's fair to say they are the best typology books, anywhere, anyhow. Take my book *Style Wars*, called trendy and metropolitan at the time, but if you look at the roster of subjects in it, they are actually more relevant now than they were then. There's a certain longevity about books. They preserve things. **99**

Ghostwriters

There are many people out there who have a very saleable name, or a saleable story to tell, but can't write. Equally, there are many writers who are perfectly capable but can't seem to make it on their own, in their own voice. When one meets the other, usually through the offices of an editor, the writer becomes a ghostwriter, and the story gets told. There are various degrees of ghostwriting, as Emma Dally explains:

66 As an editor I rewrote Lena Kennedy's first novel. Every editor restructures and rewrites and doesn't get paid for it. It's part of the job. I must say, though, once you've done it and got a percentage, then you realize how much editors are exploited. I still rewrite what Lena Kennedy writes, but I now get paid a very large sum of money to do it.

'Then there's true ghosting, which I did with *Surrogate Mother: One Woman's Story*. I started from scratch. She used to come and see me every week; I interviewed her, transcribed the tape and wrote the book. My name is on the spine. I think more and more ghosts are coming out and getting credit. like Denise Winn who wrote the Kim Cotton book, *Baby Cotton: For Love and Money*. Denise did it really quickly and got paid a large amount, whereas I did it slowly, and got paid £10,000 plus 25% of the author's royalty. And that was all down to my agent, Felicity Bryan. I had a hunch the book would be big because I was aware of the Warnock Report, and I had been working with Dame Josephine Barnes, an eminent gynaecologist. If you are an anonymous ghost, it's something that you have to be very grown-up about. **99**

WRITING POETRY

Poetry is at once the most universal and most elusive sort of writing. Most readers would agree that a poem is the most perfect and concentrated of verbal expressions, yet at any time probably more people *think* of themselves as poets than any other kinds of writer; and at the same time, poetry publishing, even in paperback, remains something of a coterie pursuit. One of the people in the middle is Andrew Motion, a practising poet published by Penguin, and, as editorial director of Chatto & Windus, responsible for their poetry list.

66 About thirty manuscripts come into Chatto unsolicited every week. As editor, you have to put yourself into the position of reading them according to what they intend to do rather than what you yourself wish to see. Even when they're unsuccessful by their own lights, there's always something interesting, or touching, thank goodness—otherwise it really would be hard work! But the number that are good, even by their own lights, is extremely small.

'When I was starting out writing poetry fifteen or so years ago, I was told by publishers that I had to establish some sort of reputation in magazines before they would consider taking a collection. That remains true to an extent. Publishing poems in magazines is obviously a way of advertising your own existence and getting the imprimatur of those editors, but if a poet were to send me a publishable manuscript of unpublished poems, I would be thrilled to bits. I know Craig Raine at Faber feels the same. The more of a reputation a new writer already has, of course, the more we're likely to pay, but I'm afraid that amount is never going to be very much: £500 and upwards in advance, and poets ought to be able to expect the normal hardback royalty of 10%, and $7\frac{1}{2}$% on a paperback. Don't be tempted by so-called vanity publishing. You get no editorial advice or guarantee of distribution. Vanity publishers collect their money at the outset; then why should they bother to sell the books? Whereas commercial publishers like us take writers on as a risk, and we have to sell them. I'm pleased when we sell 3,000 copies of a first book. Douglas Dunn will sell 20,000, Ted Hughes and Seamus Heaney about the same, I'd guess. Philip Larkin sells 25,000. But my impression, gained from sitting here for three years reading poetry is that very many more people write it than read it.

'I don't want to say that you can only write a good modern poem if you're reading a lot of good modern poetry—but it sure helps. Strong feeling isn't necessarily enough. Poets should revise a lot. The spontaneous overflow is not necessarily the best kind of overflow. And read a lot. People think poetry is expensive, but you can get a good book of poems, 50-odd pages, for £3.95—how many pints of beer can you get for that? Read a lot; revise a lot; and go to writers' groups. The Arvon Foundation at Lumb Bank and Totleigh Barton provide an excellent service. Join the Poetry Society and go to readings. Immerse yourself in living poetry as much as possible. It helps to generate a sense of society in what can be rather a solitary occupation. **99**

One poet who agrees absolutely on the importance of 'a sense of society' is Steve Turner. He says:

66 I mostly send my poetry to popular magazines rather than poetry magazines, because I feel there's a tendency for poetry to get very insular—poets just writing for other poets. Back in 1974 I'd had poems published in magazines like *Rolling Stone, Cosmopolitan*, the *Sunday Times* and others; and I approached Charisma Records, who had a book publishing company then, and persuaded them to publish a collection of my poems: *Tonight We Will Fake Love*. Surprisingly, it sold very well. Since then I've had two others out: *Nice and Nasty* and *Up To Date*. Many poets want a book out with their name on the spine, but they don't take into consideration who they are writing for, or who's reading. I urge poets to get involved in poetry readings, and not just for each other.

'When I write, it's a single line that comes to my mind first, like an opening sentence or a hook-line in a song. That line becomes the foundation stone of the poem: it suggests the next line, which suggests the next line, and so on. But I don't believe in waiting for inspiration. You have to siphon *all* the material out of your head. Some of it is bad, some of it is good. You have to remember that to write good stuff, you have to write some bad stuff.

'I think poets should read other poets. It's useful because it reminds you of how other people say things, and it sets a standard. If you just read good poets, you can get very intimidated; but reading bad poets is encouraging. You think, I could do better than that! **99**

There are some poets who make a living entirely out of performance, disdaining the traditional publication of 'slim volumes', with all their implications of a discreet and modest art. Joolz, queen of the rock poets, has released a live record of her poetry, *Never Never Land.*

❝When I was twelve, I was very ambitious, but I never sat down and thought: I want to be a poet. It's just something that I did. It came out of me and I wrote it down. I remember writing poems in my school rough book, and I used to get long demented poems in the school magazine.

'I once sent my poems off to an established poet, and he wrote back saying, "Try writing about what you know." That's always stuck with me. It's common sense. Now I always write about things or feelings I understand; or something I can research and understand. For instance, *Musket, Fife and Drum* is a poem about a soldier in the peacekeeping force in Lebanon. This young guy cracked up one day and shot three of his mates. I researched the story and then wrote the poem. It's just a case of somebody being needled by his mates, and then going crazy and lashing out at them; except that this guy happened to have a gun, and he'd been trained to kill. People come up to me and say, "Oh, I just know exactly how he felt."

'I certainly make a living out of my poetry, a very good living. Six years ago I'd just left my husband and I was very poor, and had no chance of getting a job, especially in Bradford. So I returned to poetry. I gathered a following by sheer bloody hard work: trailing around every single grotty little club or pub or fete that would have me, for years and years. I used to go up to a rock band and say, "Look, you've got a changeover between the two bands. The changeover takes ten minutes. Give me five of them."

'There is no way in other than working really hard. You have to be utterly dedicated and willing to sacrifice *everything*. You have to go on stage and be prepared to be barracked. Only last week I got a black eye at Glasgow when somebody threw a bottle at me. I was reciting poetry and they were screaming and throwing missiles at me all night. I thought: "You're not going to get me off this stage."

'Three-quarters of my gigs are abroad. I play Norway a lot, for some reason. Unlike John Cooper Clarke, who recites very quickly, I recite slowly, and if there is a difficult or slang English word, I will simplify it for foreigners. I've just done a tour in Vancouver, and I thought, God, nobody will have heard of me. But I couldn't believe it: they treated me like David Bowie. My single was number one there for ten weeks, and they had shopfronts displaying my album!

'I mostly do live work, but I've always wanted to do a book, in a certain way: with photographs and illustrations. Several publishers have asked me to do a book but they all want a slim volume of verse. I don't want that. I've just signed a deal with Virgin Books to do the book that I want to do. The big publishers just haven't got the imagination.

'I find all that literary in-crowd intensely dull and utterly irrelevant. There's an awful lot of snobbery. If you go to the right parties and say, "Darling, I just *loved* your last work, I thought the classical pun in the third stanza was absolutely *divine*," then you get on. It's a mafia. The established poets are scared stiff of anybody rocking the boat. I would defy Craig Raine to stand on that stage at Glasgow. What they have done is put poetry into an ivory tower, and that's wrong. Poetry is for everyone.

'I write whenever the mood takes me. I don't have a brain, I have a camera and a computer. I collect a mass of pictorial, factual and spoken information. I see, hear and watch everything, and write it down in little notebooks with a biro. Then I usually sit down about 2 or 3 a.m., and fit it all together like a jigsaw. Then I go over it and over it until it's ready.

'For me, though, the real thrill is the power of being on stage and being able to make people laugh or cry. I've been in front of a thousand people and had them all deathly silent except for the odd sniffle.

'I'm proud of being a poet. I've got it on my passport. If you've got the gift, you should use it. **"**

The Poetry Society
21 Earls Court Square
London SW5 9DE
(01) 373 7861

The National Book League
Book House
45 East Hill
London SW18 2QZ
(01) 870 9055

Middle England Poetry Services
Coles Lane
Sutton Coldfield
W. Midlands

Services for the poet

The Association of Little Presses
89a Tetherton Road
London N5 2QT
(01) 226 2657

The Arts Council Poetry Library
105 Piccadilly
London W1V 0AU
(01) 629 9495

The Poetry Society holds poetry forums regularly, and will put you in touch with forums in your area. They will also arrange for your poems to be criticized in detail. This service costs £17 for members and £23 for non-members for poems under 200 lines. Local poetry workshops are an excellent source of information and feedback from other poets; many publish and circulate their own magazines. Middle England Poetry Services publish contributions from subscribers to their quarterly magazine *Pause* (£7 a year, £4 for students); and instead of rejection slips, they send a critical appraisal. The Association of Little Presses charges an annual subscription of £4. Its catalogue of poetry magazines cost 50p + 40p p&p. A *Guide to Literary Prizes* will cost you £1, post free, from the National Book League. For local information, contact the Literature Officer of your Regional Arts Association, and don't forget to check library and social centre noticeboards.

FILM, TV AND RADIO

While radio is pre-eminently the medium of the spoken word, in which writers may expect to be treated with some consideration because the words come first, the opposite is true of film and TV. Writers attracted by the glamour and wealth of these visual media must understand two things:

1. it costs a *lot* of money to transfer your idea from paper to screen;
2. this process involves a *lot* of people.

Film and TV are collaborative media. Your work may be the germ without which nothing would grow into being, but this is irrelevant once a producer and a director are on the job. To them the writer, if not possessed of a famous name, is about as important as the electrician. And since the lights and the camera won't work without electricity, whereas they have the writer's script in their hands and can actually do what they like with it, on set the electrician comes *before* the writer. Camera-people, light and sound engineers, actors, floor managers and wardrobe departments will all bring their particular expertise and requirements to bear on the script before and during the shooting; and afterwards the film will be edited.

Prima donnas stop reading here.

Inside Film

To inhibit you further: the business of getting a screenplay into a studio, read, accepted, put into development, shot, edited, sold and distributed is next to impossible. Partly, this is because there are still huge sums of money to be made by successful movies, so everyone who's financially involved wants a say, and every conceivable objection to a proposed project will be raised by somebody who has their own fish to fry. Inside contacts count for more than anything else.

Your only consolation is that some absolutely *terrible* films do get made, and some of them do make money. If your work has a clear commercial angle, it stands a chance of attracting someone's attention, no matter what its quality, no matter how ruined it will be in production.

Putting a Film Together

The days of the old Hollywood studio system, when studios employed teams of screenplay writers to turn out vehicles for the company stars, are long gone. Screenwriting *is* a market for the freelance.

Studios and film companies rarely produce many more than a dozen pictures a year. They receive far more unsolicited scripts than they can handle, let alone commission works that never reach production. *But* what they do do is *develop* many more scripts than they need, in order to keep their options open and see how the market shapes up. If a star becomes available, they need to have a project for him or her. If a bandwagon starts rolling, they need a property with which to jump on board.

Planning meetings are held to discuss *properties* (which already exist) and *ideas* (which may be no more than that). As a novice, you're better off working out an idea than a complete script. Nevertheless, your idea is unlikely to be treated seriously unless it comes in the form of a proposal, complete synopsis and sample scene. The business of films, even this short way in, is so complex that you really do need an agent to sell your idea, though getting an agent for film work is even harder than getting a literary agent. If you've got this far alone, getting an agent should be less difficult, but is no less necessary. Once a company is interested in your idea, or in a property which they can mine for ideas, they will pay you a large advance, and you are in development.

At any time from Day One onwards you can be out of development. This is unlikely to mean you have to pay the cash back. There are many writers who have spent whole careers writing screenplays and never had anything reach the screen. Failure at this level is so common and intrinsic a part of the business that it counts as success. Don't get angry or depressed, just pick up the cheque, pick up your pen, and get started on the next one.

If you've already written a complete script before submitting it to a film company script department, you may receive a release form to sign before they'll read it. The point and purport of this is that they have so many scripts under consideration at any time that the chances of ideas, situations and characters coming up more than once are quite high. The release form states that you realize this, and will not immediately accuse them of piracy if a film somewhat resembling your script ever appears.

Sometimes script departments are so inundated with work that they return unsolicited material unopened. This may seem outrageous, but consider: it's better than rejecting it *pretending* they've read it. And it leaves you free to try it on them again later.

Scripts that *do* get read are read by professional readers who do nothing but read scripts all day, putting comments on any that are going on to be considered by the script department executives. *All* screenplay readers want to be screenplay writers.

There are as many routes from here as there are individual scripts. No script will ever be accepted without discussion and revision, first with the company executives, and then with producers (who may have little or no aesthetic sense, only business sense), directors (who have their own careers to consider) and stars (who are going to *be* your characters in the public mind, and so have very definite ideas about what they can and cannot say). You will find yourself doing rewrites, and rewrites, and more rewrites, often right up to the minute of shooting a scene; or until you're fired and other would-be screenwriters are brought in to rewrite your original for you!

If you are very, very lucky, the script you wrote will become a film. It won't still be the script you wrote. But you will be infinitely richer.

Success Stories

Sylvester Stallone and Rocky Sylvester Stallone was turned down by everybody in the business before United Artists took his screenplay for *Rocky* in the mid-seventies, thus engendering *Rocky II, III* and (finally?) *IV*, and earning Stallone enormous fame and wealth. *Rocky IV* took $60m in its first three weeks.

Rocky dialogue is not exactly complex or subtle; nor is the *Rocky* storyline: underdog boxer from Philadelphia overcomes everything life can throw at him and wins. Winning is still and always the American dream. Hollywood is back once again as the capital of the movie world, and Hollywood does not make blockbusting movies about losers. The popularity of self-doubt in the cinema of the sixties is over and done. Stallone sensed that America, as a nation, was shedding the embarrassments of Watergate and Vietnam. Under Reagan, it no longer felt corrupt or guilty; in fact, it began to feel muscular and proud again.

During the Vietnam war, Stallone was teaching PE at a girls' school in Switzerland. This didn't stop him producing, directing and starring in 1985's *First Blood II: Rambo*, the story of the unstoppable Vietnam vet who goes back to rescue stranded American POWs. *Rambo*, like *Rocky*, provided a new cinematic myth for the renaissance of macho America; and did pretty well in Britain too. Not that Stallone's film career has always been solid box-office gold. He prefers to forget *F.I.S.T.* and *Paradise Alley*, two films about working class heroes who grunt a lot, one in the Union and the other in Hell's Kitchen, New York, c.1940.

'I watch *Paradise Alley* at home sometimes, and have to look at it with one eye,' he says. Stallone wrote it, directed it, starred in it, sang in it, and 'received the worst reviews since Hitler'. His mistake? 'The character I portrayed should have been lively, effervescent, part of the ensemble. But instead of being the supplier of the energy, I was just the foul spark, spluttering.'

George Miller and Mad Max George Miller was in his final
year at the University of New South Wales Faculty of
Medicine when his younger brother roped him in to collabo-
rate on an entry for a student film competition. Their one-
minute movie won first prize: a course at a film workshop in
Melbourne, where Miller met and worked with Byron
Kennedy on a couple of short films. Afterwards Kennedy
continued in the film industry, while Miller went back, took
his degree, and began as an intern at St. Vincent's Hospital in
Sydney, still writing screenplays at weekends. A Kennedy-
Miller collaboration called *Violence in the Cinema—Part
One* was shown at festivals in Sydney and Moscow, and won
two awards from the Australian Film Institute.

Mad Max, produced by Kennedy and co-written by Miller
and James McCausland, was their first feature film. Released
in 1979, it won six Australian Film Institute Awards and the
Jury Prize at the Avoriaz Film Festival in France. *Time*
magazine listed it among the year's ten best pictures. In two
years it had grossed $100m. Not bad for a little film that took
nine weeks and cost $400,000 to make. 'In the first film, Max
was a cop,' explains Miller, 'a relatively normal guy with a
young family, in a degenerate world. When those closest to
him were killed, he descended into the dark side.' In fact, the
film reveals very little about Max's world and time, but for a
decrepit police station. For the sequel, *Mad Max 2*, released
two years later, Miller was able to fill in some of the
background: a post-holocaust Australian outback where, in
the words of critic Phil Hardy, 'Petrol has become the golden
commodity in a skeletal society still slavishly attached to its
automobile culture.'

Miller co-wrote *Mad Max 2* with Brian Hannant and
Terry Hayes, who recalls: 'George asked how I'd like to write
a script with him. I said I didn't know the first thing about
scriptwriting. He said that was okay. Later I realized *he*
didn't know anything about it either!'

Terry Hayes learnt a lot about the difference between the
American and Australian film industries when time came for
a third film, *Mad Max: Beyond the Thunderdome*. He says: 'In
Hollywood there is an institutionalized form of conflict. The
writer fights to defend his work against the director; the
director fights the producer; and the producer fights the
studio. In Australia, you get a chance not to be a writer or a
director. You get a chance to be a film-maker.' He and
George Miller also took the opportunity to develop the
character of Max away from being merely 'Mad'. Star Mel
Gibson observes that in *Mad Max 2*, 'Max was a sort of
closet human being. In *Thunderdome*, his protective layers
are peeled away. There's a lot more depth, variety and
humanity to the man.' The script is also remarkable for its
successful reproduction of the mutant languages of the
fractured civilization: a challenge for any writer to make
both credible and comprehensible.

Writing for Film

rules to remember

One. Keep it simple. It's no accident that the plots of both the *Rocky* and *Mad Max* films could be written, as the old adage says, on a postcard. Your story must come across in something between seventy and ninety minutes, a lot of which will be establishing shots, action sequences, meaningful close-ups, etc. etc. And with a film, unlike a book, you can't flick back to the beginning to check what's been happening. Film companies want a simple, strong storyline.

Two. Have a strong opening scene. Make sure something visual and grabby happens quickly. Though the eventual film may start out more slowly, or somewhere else altogether, the very beginning of your script is the part that's certain to get read. Make sure it stands out from the dull ones, of which the beginning is the only part that gets read.

Three. A screenplay derives its texture from its pacing; its narrative relies on regular, rhythmic change: of circumstances, character, setting, mood. Don't let it flag or flatten.

Four. Far more than a novel, a movie will sell—and be talked about—in terms of wonderful moments. Make sure you provide plenty (but not too many) of moments: confrontations, cliff-hangers, ironic deflations, breath-taking revelations...

Five. Be economic with dialogue. It's better to have a few strong, memorable lines than paragraphs of fine writing.

Six. Be ruthless. If a line, a scene or a whole character seems weak, or can't be seen to be integral to the play, cut it out.

Presenting a Script

You have an idea, characters, a plot. You now have to present these visual elements verbally, through dialogue and briefly-described action. The pitfalls for the novice are many. Remember: don't pre-empt (*a*) the casting; (*b*) the costuming; (*c*) the camera direction. These are not your job. The people whose jobs they are will look much more kindly and keenly on a script which offers them a clear space to *do* those jobs than on one that's cluttered with inexpert advice.

The best way to learn to set out a script is to take a look at a real one. Movie memorabilia shops and auctions will often have dusty old copies of forgotten features that cost mere pence and can be used as a format. Basically: use one side only of good quality A4 paper; type cleanly and clearly and leave lots of space. As a rough guide, one page of script equals one minute of film time. Aim for 90 pages.

Start each scene with a number on the left. Note whether it's an exterior (EXT) or interior (INT) scene. Name the scene (THE BATHROOM; MINDY'S RESTAURANT). Keep exactly the same name for the same location when you next return to it. Note the light: DAY or NIGHT.

These three instructions form the title of the scene and are written in capital letters, e.g.

25.　EXT　　　SAMANTHA'S BEDROOM　　　NIGHT

Staging directions start at the left-hand margin. Dialogue runs down the middle of the page. Expressive directions to actors go with the dialogue, each on a line of its own, indented. All of this goes into upper and lower case.

Names of characters are written in capital letters except when they are spoken in dialogue. When they indicate who is speaking, they go on a line of their own, in the middle of the page, above the portion of dialogue. Thus:

SAMANTHA is sprawled across her bed. An empty bottle of pills lies on its side on her bedside table.
DESMOND
(softly)

Samantha—that'll teach you
to cheat on me, you bitch!

Forget about camera directions unless they are absolutely essential to describe your scene. Our scene now reads:

25.　EXT　　SAMANTHA'S BEDROOM　　　NIGHT

SAMANTHA is sprawled across her bed. An empty bottle of pills lies on its side on her bedside table.
CUT TO: CLOSE UP OF DESMOND
DESMOND
(softly)

Samantha—that'll teach you
to cheat on me, you bitch!

Tedious though it is to prepare and expensive to photocopy, this format will distinguish at once the professional mind from the star-struck innocent. The point of the layout is that different sorts of information, for different members of the cast and crew, can be located immediately. Huge margins and acres of empty white paper allow private notes, second thoughts and vital questions to be jotted down where they belong without making the thing instantly illegible.

Add your name and address to the title page and the last page. Unlike novels, filmscripts should be bound, with protective covers front and back. They're not going to be dismantled for typesetting, but they are (you hope) going to be handled by lots of people, so this does make sense. Send your script to the script department of the studio or company concerned, with the briefest of covering letters if there's any extra information (as distinct from cheery good wishes or pathetic pleas) you wish to draw their attention to. Enclose return postage. If they don't simply return the script, they should send you a formal acknowledgment. After this, give them at least two months before your polite letter or phone call asking what's happening to your work.

Television

Television differs from film in that the turnover is faster, the demand for scripts is greater, the competition, though tough, is not impossible, and the range of possible subject matter is wider. TV programmes cost much less to make than movies; but because there's less money available and deadlines are shorter, TV can be rushed, sets makeshift and effects less elaborate, especially on something by a newcomer.

British TV provides a buoyant market for good scripts of all types, and standards of production are acknowledged globally to be high, both for the IBA and BBC. The BBC provides the largest single market for the writer. Somehow, they manage to read several thousand unsolicited scripts a year, most of them quite hopeless.

For BBC, write to:
Head of Script Unit
BBC TV Centre
London W12 7RJ

For ITV, write to the Script Unit of your local Programme Contractor (Granada TV, Tyne Tees TV, etc.)—addresses in the phonebook

TV programming is divided up by categories: Drama, Light Entertainment, Current Affairs, Music, Children's, etc. Address your scripts to the Script Department in the first instance. If they feel your work shows potential, they will pass it on to the relevant department, and you will hear from a producer. Unlike films, where the producer is simply head of administration who deals with financiers, in TV producers have more to do with the making of a film. As a writer, you can expect to be dealing with them.

Rik Mayall "I wrote *The Young Ones* with Lise Mayer and Ben Elton. We wanted it to be unpredictable, exciting and outrageous and we quickly sussed out how to get around the script editors. If we wanted to put in an obscene joke, then we would put something totally outrageous on the next page. Script editors always have to cut something so you have to give them something to cut.

'I can't believe that *The Young Ones* attracted 6 million viewers every show. It amazes me. It scares me when I forget to watch TV as a practitioner—I need to have an impression of what different TV is like. 'The reason we didn't do a third series is because its unpredictability had become predictable. **99**

Plays

The recommended way for a first-time scriptwriter to get into television is to write an original play. Dramatizing somebody else's story or novel is unlikely to get you anywhere, as this work is always done by experts in-house or on commission. All TV drama producers are continually looking for good original works to fit time-slots of 90, 75, 50 and 30 minutes. (If you're aiming at ITV, don't forget to work in gaps for the commercial breaks.) Plays are in any case ideal for the beginner, because they're works which show producers and script editors that you can conceive, develop and conclude a piece of writing properly.

The BBC state that 'any subject or setting is acceptable, and the best rule for a writer to follow is to write the sort of play he would like to see on screen'. Having said that, they will of course reserve the right to reject any ideas they find too politically sensitive, damaging to their dignity, offensive to public morality, etc. etc. You'll be very much better guided by what sort of plays are currently broadcast in the slot you're aiming at. Don't look for a formula to copy, but don't do anything too out of keeping either. And be realistic. Show them that you can anticipate and work within budget constraints. Car chases through Heathrow will be less attractive to them than two travellers stuck in a station waiting room.

Comedy

The most lucrative sort of TV scriptwriting is the situation comedy series ('M.A.S.H.', 'Fawlty Towers', 'Only Fools and Horses'), where a group of strong and strongly-contrasted characters are thrown together in any situation that will provide half-an-hour's laughter every week. The acceptable form for selling a sitcom is a proposal, script for a pilot episode, and synopses for five more episodes. But you're unlikely to start off in TV with a comedy series, or indeed a series of any kind, except in collaboration with an established writer. The sharpest comedy writing often comes from partnerships, each acting as a check on whether the other's ideas are actually funny.

The business of writing TV comedy is actually very serious and businesslike. Precision of timing and nuance, and accuracy of construction matter more in comedy than any other kind of broadcast writing. It's a profession to be learnt. The usual apprenticeship, unless you're a member of the Cambridge Footlights Revue, is to train on short material, from one-line gags to six-minute sketches, for programmes like *The Two Ronnies* or *Benny Hill*.

presenting a script

Read *Writing for the BBC* (available from P.O. Box 234, London SE1 3TH) and *BBC TV Script Requirements* (from the Script Unit, address above)

The layout of a TV script is similar to that of a filmscript, except that stage directions are always written in capital letters, and the dialogue all runs down the right-hand side of the page only. Leave a 4" margin on the left for the producer, director, crew and cast to scribble their own annotations. Here are two specimen scripts: the first from *Writing for the BBC* and the second from one I worked on with Bernard Taylor for a comedy series, *Mother, it's Me.*

40.   INT.   .   MILNE'S OFFICE.   DAY.

(WITH THE CLOCK AT 10.30, THE MINISTERIAL PARTY HAS ARRIVED. THEY ENTER THE OFFICE, ALL SMILES, TO BE GREETED BY A SMILING STEAD AND MILNE.

THE MARTIAL MUSIC BLARES INANELY ON)

TELECINE 17:
The pipeline. Day.

41.   INT.   MILNE'S OFFICE.   DAY.

(EVERYBODY IS LAUGHING AND DRINKING. THE CLOCK SAYS 10.45. MILNE STARTS USHERING PEOPLE TO THE DOOR)

TELECINE 18:

Ext. Refinery. Day. THORNTON roars in to the refinery, martial music drifting across the storage tanks, and turns off the valve. The sound of the pump motor stops.

42.   INT.   MILNE'S OFFICE.   DAY.

(PEOPLE ARE PUTTING DOWN THEIR GLASSES AND GETTING READY TO MOVE)

STEAD: Ladies and gentlemen, if you'll kindly come this way, we're about to start.

(BUT AT THIS MOMENT THE DOOR OPENS AND THORNTON RUSHES IN)

STEAD: Peter!

THORNTON: Quiet, everybody, please. You must leave the refinery immediately. There's a bomb ...

MOTHER, IT'S ME

1.   INT.   ROME OFFICE.   DAY.

BIG DESK, SEVERAL PHONES. AWARDS ON THE WALLS. WINDOW LOOKING OUT OVER ROME SCENE. JANE, DISTRESSED AND AGITATED, PUTS DOWN THE PHONE. SHE IS MID-THIRTIES, ELEGANTLY DRESSED.

OLAF LARSEN ENTERS. HE IS SWEDISH, GOOD LOOKING. EARLY TO MID-FORTIES. DRESSED CASUALLY BUT SMART.

OLAF:
So what's happening?

JANE:
They're getting me a taxi. I shall have to go home and pack right away. I'm leaving at four o'clock.

OLAF:
Are you flying?

JANE:
Yes, of course.

OLAF:
By plane?

JANE:
No, by balloon. Of course by plane.

OLAF:
Don't be upset.

JANE:
What d'you mean, don't be upset?! She's my mother. Of course I'm upset. I'm all she's got in the world. Can't you understand?—she's ill.

OLAF:
How was she the last time you saw her?

JANE:
She was fine. But that was three years ago. Three years! I haven't set eyes on my poor little widowed mother in all that time. (GETTING TEARFUL) Sometimes I miss her so much!

The successful screenwriter John Cleese: 66 At school I was always in the bottom 25% for English, which is odd, seeing as I earn my living as a writer. I think I had the ability, but it was never recognized from my essays.

'When I started in TV, I realized instinctively that to be able to do the sort of comedy that I liked, I would have to serve my apprenticeship, doing shows like *The Frost Report*, which were successful and very good of their kind, but didn't take risks. We used to suggest crazy things, but the producer would smile nicely, shake his head, and say: "Yes, but they wouldn't understand it in Bradford." He always used that phrase.

'*Monty Python's Flying Circus* was very risky, and I'm proud of the risks we took. I remember distinctly standing in the dressing room with Michael Palin ten minutes before we started and saying to him: "You do realize that we could perform the next hour to complete silence." And then we went out there. The most exciting moment was about four minutes into the first show, when people started to giggle and we realized that we weren't wrong, that the show was going to appeal to somebody.

'I find writing easier these days. Not because I'm any better, but because I've learnt what the process of writing is all about. When I used to get stuck I would panic. Then I came to realize that the blocked periods are as much part of the process of writing as the periods of actual writing. Gregory Bateson said, "You can't really have a new thought until you've got rid of an old one," which I think sounds a very clumsy, chemical way of thinking, but I do think he's right. A period when you're blocked is when you've got a thought which doesn't work, and you can't quite move it to make space for the next one. So now if I'm stuck, I just accept that I'm stuck. I can make it very much better by starting projects very early, so that I can be stuck without a feeling of pressure. Like the party political broadcast for the SDP: within a week of taking it on, I did a draft. Very rough. Then I got everyone's comments and in the light of that did a second draft, and then got more comments and did a third draft.

'The other advantage of writing like that is your structure becomes foremost. I've picked up so many comedy scripts in the last fifteen years that have had beautifully written stage directions and dialogue for ten pages, then fall apart. The last ten pages are rushed, badly thought out and unfunny. You realize that they started page one writing as if that was going to be page one of the fourth draft.

'There's no point in writing like that—and I say that genuinely to anybody who's thinking of writing. Always do it rough. The thing is to get the shape right. Once you get the shape right and the plot right, then everything else is easy. But you can't do that to begin with because it's too big a vision.

'If you concentrate on getting the first bit right and then the second bit right, the chances of getting it *all* right are nil. If you start doing it rough, you can see what it's all about, and what the plot's going to be, and what relation one person is to another. Also, if you put all the best jokes in the first ten pages you soon dry up.

'Writing has got easier for me, and I've become more skilful and experienced at knowing what works and what doesn't, but I don't think I've got any more creative. I've also got much better at cutting, because for the first ten years you write, cutting a line is like cutting off a limb. But you're always better to cut. When in doubt, cut, cut, cut. **99**

Radio

local radio

The best place to start writing for radio is not at the top, with the national network of the BBC, but at your local radio station. Local radio is desperate for ideas and material, and welcomes approaches from creative people in the immediate locality. Because they are committed to serving their area, topics and issues of local concern will always receive priority of attention, so you'd be well advised to exploit that. If you're trying your hand at a soap opera or comedy series, set it in a local town. Tie your short story in to some current development or piece of local history.

Once you've approached a producer and penetrated the offices of the station, you'll find the atmosphere much more relaxed and informal than within the corridors of national radio (let alone TV) where, the pressure is always on.

Contact your Independent Local Radio station directly; or write for general information to the Association of Independent Radio Contractors
Regina House
259 Old Marylebone Road
London SW3 1EY

the BBC

The BBC itself gets through an enormous number of scripts weekly, especially for Radios 3 and 4, where opportunities vary from documentary to satire. Three possibilities you may consider are comedy, short stories and plays.

Comedy

Rules for radio comedy are much the same as for TV, with, if anything, a more stringent emphasis on polish and precision. The only thing that the process of broadcasting can add to your material is timing and delivery. Sound comedy is purely verbal, so the words must be right. Take a tip from comedian Les Dawson, who noticed early on in his career that certain words are potentially funny, while others, almost the same in meaning, are not. Les compiled himself a list in two columns: *notice* is not funny, *placard* is; *coach* is not, *charabanc* is . . . The sound value or connotations of an otherwise innocent word may tip the comic balance.

That said, there are many many things which aren't a bit funny written down, but read out by the right people with exactly the right intonation could well be. The result of this, for the novice radio comedy writer, is that script readers and editors often query or reject jokes that look flat on the page unless they come from established and trusted writers. As in so much freelance writing, the incentive is to be sharper and funnier and better than the professionals. Douglas Adams was already a professional working in broadcasting, but not at all a famous writer, when he wrote *The Hitch-Hiker's Guide to the Galaxy: The Original Radio Scripts*, now published by Pan. The scripts have polish and precision aplenty (which the four later novel versions simply don't). They also demonstrate the immense importance of using sound effects inventively. Douglas Adams made more exciting and exasperating demands upon the BBC effects department than any radio writer since Spike Milligan.

Saleable comic writing can be anything from topical one-liners for *Weekending* to whole ideas (proposal, pilot and synopses) for new comic series. Comedy scripts are handled by the Light Entertainment Department.

Short stories

Writing a short story for radio is much the same as writing one for a magazine or anthology, with the obvious proviso that hearing a story read is not the same as reading it for yourself. In general:

- Avoid long, complexly-subordinated sentences.

- Avoid confusing time-sequences. Signal flashbacks, etc. clearly and distinctly. ('It was in the previous spring that I had first met Norman . . .')

- Avoid abstraction. Internal monologues of solitary characters reflecting on life and the world are perfectly all right, but radio offers you a unique appeal to the listener's *visual* imagination. Radio audiences want and expect to have things conjured up vividly for them.

- Don't be afraid of repeating visual information, e.g. who each character is if there are more than three of them. ('Frank tried to phone *his sister* Hazel, but she had already left for the day.')

As a rough guide, a fifteen-minute story should not be more than 2,500 words. The names of producers of *Morning Story*, etc., are announced at the end of the broadcast.

Read
Notes on Radio Drama
available from the
Script Editor,
Drama Radio,
BBC Broadcasting
House,
Portland Place,
London W1A 1AA

Plays

The BBC buys a large number of radio plays, and it's here, as for TV, that you'd do well to start. All remarks on writing plays for TV apply, except, most importantly, that for radio a play with a car chase through Heathrow is no problem at all, and is probably a better bet commercially than one set entirely in a station waiting room. In the preface to her collection *Come unto these Yellow Sands* (published by Bloodaxe Books), Angela Carter explains:

66 Radio can move from location to location with effortless speed, using aural hallucinations to invoke sea-coast, a pub, a blasted heath, and can make extraordinary collage and montage effects beyond the means of any film-maker, not just because of the cost of that medium but also because the eye takes longer to register changing images than does the ear...
'In a radio drama studio, the producer, the actors, the technical staff, create an illusion, literally, out of the air. Although there is a beautiful precision about the means available for the creation of that illusion. If you want to invoke a windy day on radio, you can specify just what kind of wind you want. Every wind in the world is stored away in the sound archives, somewhere on a disc. **99**

Angela Carter is one of the most inventive and original of radio dramatists, and this book of four of her scripts is well worth studying, not only for the variety, vitality and colour of the kinds of dialogue and monologue she creates, but also for her sense of *space*. By the simple use of different acoustics, she can switch from a market in Cairo where part of her story takes place, to another level where the character is reflecting on what happened there. It's a mark of her skill that there's never any confusion between the various scenes and levels of the play. Radio can open and close whole areas of narrative at the touch of a switch. You too can make use of that, and of anything that can be done in accompanying sound effects and music so that your characters don't have to explain to each other where they are and what they're doing.

presenting a script

Number each speech on the left, starting with number 1 for the first speech on each page. Then give the name of the speaker in full, in capital letters, followed by a colon. Expressive directions to actors follow, inside brackets, typed in upper and lower case and underlined. Type dialogue in upper and lower case, leaving a left-hand margin large enough for the character with the longest name.

A speech ends when a new speaker takes over, or when a sound effect is described. Sound effects run in line with the dialogue, inside brackets, in capital letters and underlined. What follows is a new speech, with a new number; if the same character is speaking, use ditto marks in the margin instead of repeating the name. If a speaker continues over the turning on a page, mark '/NAME cont'd...' at the bottom right-hand corner on the page, and '1. NAME cont'd:' in the margin by the resumption of the speech on the next page.

All of these points are illustrated in the following sample script from Angela Carter's 1982 Monday Play 'Puss in Boots'.

Page 1 _____

6. PUSS:	Tabs, my dearest ... slowly re-capitulate for me the daily motions of Signor Pantaleone, alias old Pantaloon, when he's at home. *(FADE IN CHURCH BELL RINGING FOUR AS TABS SPEAKS)*
7. TABS:	*(Narrating)* They set the clock of the duomo by him, so rigid and regular is he in his habits. Up at the crack— *(COCK-CROW; PANTALEONE MAKES WAKING-UP GRUNTS)*
8. " :	He makes a meagre breakfast off yesterday's crusts... *(GNAWING AT STALE BREAD)*
9. PANTALEONE:	*(IN ROOM ACOUSTIC)* ... bread's tough, this morning...
10. TABS:	...which he dips to soften 'em in a cup of cold water— *(WATER POURED OUT)*
	TABS cont'd...

Page 2

1. TABS: cont'd	that he drinks cold, to spare the expense of a fire. Then, bright and early, down to the counting-house—
2. PANTALEONE:	Good morrow to my gold!
3. TABS:	—counting out the money— *(CHINK, CHINK, CHINK; PANTALEONE GIGGLES AND BABBLES WITH GLEE)*
4. " :	until a well-earned bowl of water gruel, that is, water extravagantly *boiled*, served hot—
5. PANTALEONE:	*(Smacks lips)* That's the stuff!
6. TABS:	—at midday. His afternoons he devotes to usury, bankrupting here—
7. SMALL TRADESMAN:	I'm ruined. You devil!
8. TABS:	—a small businessman; there, a weeping widow.
9. WIDOW:	My starving children! My roofless orphans!

INDEX